THE ART OF
BREATHING

THE ART OF
BREATHING

Nancy Zi

Vivi Co.

Vivi Company
Glendale, California

THE ART OF BREATHING

A Vivi Book January 1997

Designed by Compage, San Francisco, California

Edited by Gail Larrick
Book design by Joy Dickinson
Ilustrations by Eric Maché
Cover design by Lightbourne Images

Library of Congress Catalog Card number 96-60745

ISBN 1-884872-72-7 (Previously ISBN 1-884872-62-X)

Vivi Books and videos are published by the Vivi Company, P.O. Box 750,
Glendale, California 91209-0750, USA

NOTE: *An earlier version of* The Art of Breathing, *without the companion video, was published by Bantam Books as part of the Bantam New Age Books series. A second edition was revised to coordinate with a self-paced video,* The Art of Breathing. *This revised and expanded third edition contains a fourth part and an extended epilogue.*

PRINTED IN THE UNITED STATES OF AMERICA

9 8 7 6 5 4 3

*This book is dedicated
to my mother,
Mrs. Lucy Ma Zi,
and my late father,
Reverend Dr. Benjamin Dung Hwe Zi*

Caution

This or any exercise program may result in injury. Please consult your doctor before beginning this or any exercise program. The exercises, instructions, and advice in this program are in no way intended as a substitute for medical counseling.

QUANTITY DISCOUNTS are available on bulk purchases to **Schools**, **Corporations**, and **Professional Organizations** using this book for training, fund raising, or other volume needs. For information contact: Marketing Department, Vivi Company, P.O. Box 750, Glendale, CA 91209-0750 U.S.A.; or, call 1-800-INHALE-8 (1-800-464-2538)/1-818-500-8889; or, send a FAX to 1-818-507-6638.

Acknowledgments

I wish to express my deepest appreciation to Mr. Wang Chi Chien for writing the calligraphic Chinese characters that so beautifully adorn the part openers of this book and its companion video.

My heartfelt thanks must go to:

Mr. Ernie Pereira, retired managing editor of the *Hong Kong Standard* daily newspaper, who gave me the first words of encouragement and guidance in beginning this book.

Professor and Mrs. John Hsu of Cornell University, whose wise suggestions and careful scrutiny have led this book onto a much wiser course.

Sue Yung Li Ikeda for invaluable artistic advise and other counsel.

Eric Maché for his ingenious illustrations and Melanie Maché for being such a patient model.

Charles Hammond and Margaret M. Meier in preparing the original manuscript.

My daughter, Violette Li Huang, for her tireless effort and talented support in facilitating every facet of this project.

My son, Vincent Li, for his silent encouragement that mom has much more to give before signing off.

Gail Larrick for her invaluable guidance and for being the miraculous editor who has nurtured this book from beginning to the present.

Flo Selfman for her most effective and resourceful public relations talent. Without her loving and caring participation, this book may not have been as readily known to you.

Gloria Balcom for her fantastic business management and multi-faceted talent. She truly is a precious guiding light.

I cannot thank Alan Freeland and Kenneth Burke enough. Without them, this book would never have materialized.

It goes without saying that above all, my hustand, S. Paul Li's fullest understanding and support of my mission to spread the goodness of the art of breathing have made the pursuance of this project possible. THANK YOU!

Praise for The Art of Breathing

"A must for anyone who wants to feel better, ease daily stresses, and have the energy to propel them through the day."
— Jack Canfield, co-author, *Chicken Soup for the Soul*

"An important book in teaching us how to properly breathe."
— Dr. Earl Mindell, author, *The Vitamin Bible*, *The Anti-Aging Bible*

"For the first time in months, I felt a deep sense of relaxation—in touch with my forgotten 'breath of life.'"
— Ray Sahelian, M.D., author, *Melatonin: Nature's Sleeping Pill*

"We in the entertainment industry are in the business of creating illusions. But the very real benefits to be derived from *The Art of Breathing* are no illusion. I heartily recommend it for actors, singers, writers, and anyone else seeking tranquility, focus, and renewed energy."
— Robert Wise, Academy Award-winning director, *West Side Story, The Sound of Music*

"With *The Art of Breathing*, tensions are released and the body becomes a conduit for a liberated stream of creativity."
— Natalie Limonick, Professor of Music; President, Opera Guild of Southern California

"From its first appearance on our shelves, *The Art of Breathing* quickly became a standard. We recommend it enthusiastically to our customers who request a book or video on breathing."
— Mary Kara, Owner, The Psychic Eye Book Shops, Inc., The Country's Largest New Age Book Stores

"Zi gives us one of the most thorough and lucid presentations on the health of good breathing. Plenty of visuals, [clear] instructions...A sensible method of getting up (doing *chi yi* exercises) that gets the energy juices flowing better than coffee."
— The Book Reader

"Nancy Zi has given us a masterpiece in her health program... the video exercises [are] invigorating, easy to follow, based on simplicity and results...Nancy's narration throughout the video is smooth and concise, obviously tempered through many years of teaching and training." — Whole Life Times

"Both the book and the video are excellent sources. I am unaware of any other book that provides such practical and thorough instructions on *how* to do [the exercises]...Nancy Zi is an inspiring teacher."
— The Georgia Strait, Vancouver, B.C.

"Ms. Zi...is lively and appealing...This video is very highly recommended." — Awareness Magazine

"Easy to learn and a joy to incorporate into daily life...Perfect for singers. Highly recommended." — Heartsong Review

"More than an exercise program, *The Art of Breathing* has the potential to penetrate and change all aspects of living, simply and powerfully." — NAPRA ReView

Companion Video—Now Available

Because people learn in various ways, and because we have had many requests for a video to accompany the book, a companion video for *The Art of Breathing* was produced.

The video invites you to learn how to convert your breath into inner energy current. It, like the book, is presented in six progressive lessons with imagery drills. These lessons and drills will lead you to acquire a greater sense of vitality and balance, and sharpen your mental and physical coordination. As you develop breath control and awareness through *chi yi*, you will find the principles of disciplined breathing moving effortlessly into your daily activities. The results can forever enhance your life by cultivating the power of *chi*—mental and physical health, energy level, personality, voice, coordination, athletic potential, and more.

Although the book and the video are each independently valuable, taking advantage of both simultaneously can greatly facilitate and enhance the learning process. While the book provides more background information, theoretical discussion, and detailed explanation, and it places greater emphasis on application, the video offers extensive visual aids, thus emphasizing easy execution of the exercises and imagery drills.

The book and the video provide a complete course. Mastering this course will enable you to:

- Apply *chi yi* to virtually any endeavor—athletics, theater, singing, yoga, meditation, and more.
- Reduce stress and promote relaxation, as well as combat insomnia and other physical discomforts.
- Find a common center for your mental and physical movements to produce an aura of poise, grace, and ease.
- Look, feel, and be healthier, and bounce back more quickly from illness.
- Gain increased stamina, radiance, and general well-being.

For information regarding this video, book, or book & video boxed set, contact Vivi Company, P.O. Box 750, Glendale, California 91209-0750, U.S.A., or call 1-800-INHALE-8 (1-800-464-2538) or 1-818-500-8889, or fax 1-818-507-6638.

Contents

Imagery Drills

Targeted Exercises

THE ART OF
BREATHING

A Singer's Discoveries

Breath is life. Learning to control the breath adds a new dimension of control and ease to every action, no matter how simple or how complex it is. In fact, the effectiveness of every activity we undertake—singing, walking, exercising, working, dancing, public speaking—depends greatly on how we use the air we breathe.

My voice is my career. For more than three decades, much of my time has been devoted to singing and to voice instruction. My performance schedule is extensive and my teaching schedule full. I have to make certain that my singing voice is always in good condition and that my speaking voice does not strain my vocal cords. To maintain the quality of voice I desire, effective controlled breathing is my most important tool.

During my college days, at Millikin University in Illinois, I sang in student recitals and performed in many opera productions. Deep breathing automatically accompanied me whenever I stepped onstage to sing. Then, during my junior year, I was elected a candidate for Homecoming Queen. I will never forget the parade of candidates, each of us swiveling at center stage in front of a panel of judges. Suddenly I was like a lump of clay! What had happened to my customary poise and stage presence? Years later, the answer became clear to me. My breathing technique had eluded me, and without it I also lost my vibrancy and the ability to project my personality.

In the years that followed, I learned to apply the lesson of that experience: Deep breathing can get me through most situations.

Controlled deep breathing helps the body to transform the air we breathe into energy. The stream of energized air produced by properly executed and controlled deep breathing produces a current of inner energy which radiates throughout the entire body and can be channeled to the body areas that need it the most, on demand. It can be used to fuel a specific physical effort, such as tennis or jogging. Or you can use this current of inner energy to relieve muscular tension throughout the body, revitalize a tired mind, or soothe localized aches and pains.

My years of experience in training and maintaining the human voice have convinced me that the practice of the art of breathing is beneficial to the health of the whole person, regardless of career or activity. In this book I will share with you some of the discoveries I have made as a singer and voice teacher. These experiences have made me aware of the wide applications of disciplined, effective breathing.

As my understanding of the benefits of controlled breathing developed, I began to formulate the principles of what I call *chi yi*. *Chi* means breath, air, atmosphere. Yi means art. Hence *chi yi*—the art of breathing.

Chi yi (pronounced *chee ee*), the breathing method I have developed, is influenced in part by the basic principles of the ancient Chinese art of breath manipulation known as *chi kung* (pronounced *chee gung*). For centuries, the Chinese have practiced *chi kung* as a fundamental discipline and have applied this discipline to many forms of martial arts, meditation, and healing practices. As a Western-trained singer and as a researcher and practitioner of the ancient art of *chi kung* and its related disciplines, I have compared, extracted, and compiled techniques from both East and West to create *chi yi*, a direct and concise way to teach the art of breathing. The current of inner energy that is generated as a result of my method of deep breathing is comparable to the principle of "inner vigor" upon which *chi kung is* based.

The practice of *chi kung is* concerned not only with the process of breathing and self-energizing; it also encompasses the ancient Chinese understanding of disciplined breathing as a means of acquiring total control over body and mind. It gives us physiological and psychological balance and the balance of *yin* and *yang*—a symbolic expression of such universal polarities as masculine and feminine, light and dark, creative and receptive.

In *chi yi*, that energy is manifested through the manipulation of simultaneous inward and outward muscular pressure, thus creating opposing forces. By properly balancing these forces, we allow energy to emerge.

The ancient practitioners of *chi kung* further associated the inner energy that derives from disciplined breathing with the quality and vigor of the blood. They deduced ways to control and regulate the seemingly automatic breathing function, which they saw as voluntary. By deliberately controlling the breathing process, they found that other functions of the body—heartbeat, blood flow, and many other physical and emotional functions—could be consciously altered. The mind, said *chi kung* practitioners, can control and manipulate the flow of energy that is created through proper breathing. Therefore the mind, coordinated with breathing, can be responsible for the state of one's physical health, one's blood pressure, one's immune system, and one's mental condition. A *chi kung* expert can channel the inner energy to any location in the body at will. In other words, the accomplished practitioner can "think" this inner energy to any destination in the body where it is needed.

As time went on, the philosophical aspect of *chi kung* was explored in many books, but the technical aspect was treated as a closely guarded secret. Without documentation, the words of generations of teachers and pupils varied greatly in interpretation and practice. Therefore, while *chi kung* became the foundation that teaches the manipulation of body, mind, and spirit, different schools evolved that built upon this foundation yet had very different goals. *Tai chi* and other forms of the martial arts and meditation disciplines are all related to *chi kung*.

Centuries passed, and with the advent of machinery and explosive weapons, the martial arts waned in appeal. External sources of strength and power totally overshadowed the internal energy men and women had once learned to create within their own bodies through self-discipline. The specific talent for energizing the body through disciplined breathing was neglected and nearly forgotten. Western modernization seemed to have eclipsed many of the subtle practices of the East. Today, however, a new era of physical awareness has stimulated the reexamination of Eastern culture, with its foundation based on the importance of the inner self.

In effective breathing, of course, there is no East or West. True, different cultures have placed different degrees of emphasis on the importance and development of breathing, and have called their techniques by different names. Their ultimate objective, however, is the same: to derive the maximum efficiency from the inhaled breath.

My intention in *The Art of Breathing* is not to revive or to propagate *chi kung* but to bring attention to and illustrate the existence of the power that is ours if we choose to have it. By cultivating that power through the practice of *chi yi,* we can excel in our endeavors and become more successful and dynamic people. The exercises, applications of *chi yi* principles, and imagery drills described in this book will enable you to build a solid, deep, effective breathing system to support whatever activities you pursue.

To further help you apply the infinite power of *chi yi* in your everyday life, I have added Part Four to this new edition. This 80-page expansion allows me to answer questions posed by students, workshop participants, and readers. I am grateful for their inspiration in pursuing this marvelous Question and Answer dialogue forum. My answers, some reinforced with targeted exercises, will show you new and more personalized ways to apply the benefits of *chi yi* to a cross-section of needs and activities. These 50 questions are listed in the Contents section by number and identified with a brief description to help you isolate topics of specific interest to you.

In the new Epilogue, I have taken the liberty of sharing some of my personal evolvement through more than six decades of breathing—for air, for *chi,* and for enlightenment. We know that life begins with the first breath and ends with the last. But it is *how* we breathe in between the first and the last that greatly impacts how well we live this life. This is what *The Art of Breathing* is all about.

PART ONE

The Promise of Chi Yi

Chi Yi: An Art for Today

The newborn infant gasps for its first breath, and life ends with a final exhalation. But breathing is more than just an instinct that is active from birth to death. When properly executed, breathing can help you develop to the utmost, enabling you to acquire a greater sense of power and balance and to sharpen both your mental and physical coordination. This is the promise of *chi yi*.

The demands of today's society, working conditions, and environment are complicated and frequently stressful; and our energy needs, both physical and mental, are forced to change rapidly to cope with all the forms of tension to which we are subjected. Innumerable varieties of relaxation techniques—transcendental meditation, self-hypnosis, physical exercises, biofeedback, and many others—are available today. But no matter what method is practiced, a mode of breathing in one way or another always comes into the picture.

Modern science has done wonders to elevate the standard of human existence, with the expectation that new inventions and medical discoveries will raise our physical and mental well-being to ever-higher states. Advanced education systems sharpen our minds, while vitamins and nutritional supplements ensure that our bodies are well nourished. Great efforts are devoted to developing innumerable variations of exercises that promise to enhance our physical shape and condition. All these avenues for generating and maintaining a high level of energy are pursued with the intention of producing a better, more exciting person.

Ironically, in our search for energy resources to maintain this modern lifestyle, we have overlooked the potential of the greatest energy source available to everyone: the current of vital energy that can be generated within our bodies, using the air we breathe as fuel. The Chinese call that energy *chi*.

Chi yi is a method of deep breathing through which you can stimulate and harness the current of inner energy. By making sure that the air you breathe is effectively inhaled, energized, and exhaled, you can improve your health and bring vitality to all your physical movements and expressions.

We have all experienced the direct link between our breathing and the way we feel physically and emotionally. We speak of a sigh of relief, of gasping in horror, of holding the breath in anticipation, of being breathless with excitement. Laughing, sighing, yawning, yelling, gasping, screaming—nature provides us with all these responses to help us fulfill the emotional demands of the instant. Physically, these acts provide us with the extra oxygen to meet a potential need.

These outbursts stimulate deep breathing—breathing to the "core"—in effect opening up vents to release emotional steam. In the next section, we will look at the core of our bodies—what it is, where it is located, and its role in effective breathing.

The Core

As you learn to apply the principles of *chi yi*, you will develop your core, and you will learn how to lead the breath to the point where the core is located. Your stresses, worries, anger, and other tensions will follow the stream of your breath to this center, where the core will shrink away your negative emotions—pain, fear, anxiety, anger, sadness, and even depression—leaving you ready to meet the challenges that you face.

To understand that a central core exists within all human beings is to open your eyes to a whole new dimension of your being. The core has always been within you. When it is stimulated it becomes increasingly effective. It does not grow in size, but in intensity.

The core is located at the center of the body, measuring from head to toe. That point is located approximately 2 to 5 inches below the navel (see Figure 1). The entire body is coordinated from this center of balance. In fact, this core is the center not only of your physical balance but of your mental and emotional balance as well.

The core thrives on attention and stimulation. The more you practice breathing to the core, the more energy it stores and is prepared to release, thus becoming a stronger pivot point for your physical, mental, and emotional balance and control.

In times of emotional crisis or at other crucial moments of distress or physical pain, we frequently hear the advice, "Take a deep breath and get hold of yourself." A very wise suggestion indeed, if we only knew how to make that "deep breath" effective. Expanding the chest and attempting to fill the lungs with additional air isn't necessarily helpful; the goal is to direct air deep toward the core.

It is impossible to explain in scientific terms the process of breathing to the core. Like energy, the core of a person is an abstract entity. Through exercises and imagery drills we can sense it, develop and cultivate it, manipulate it, and feel the power of its presence, but we cannot see it with our eyes.

Introducing the Imagery Drills

The following challenges to the imagination are the first of several "imagery drills," which make use of mental pictures to help you experience specific sensations or feelings in the body. These mental pictures are metaphorical descriptions of particular movements that may be otherwise impossible to describe. They communicate a muscular process indirectly, through the use of *images* of movement. Such images are useful in elucidating invisible, internal movements and subtle adjustments of the body. This brief introduction to the awareness of inner energy merely suggests the energy source you will learn to tap in the exercises and applications that follow.

These imagery drills may be difficult for those who are unaccustomed to manipulating their breathing apparatus. Many athletes, singers, and musicians who play wind instruments, for example, are conscientious breathers, and will be able to handle the drills easily. Others will need to wait until they have practiced a good number of the exercises in Part Two before being able to complete the drills correctly and with little strain.

Practice these drills as they are introduced to become familiar with the internal sensations each one stimulates. Review the drills as necessary to reestablish your awareness of a sensation.

The first of these drills, the Eyedropper Imagery Drill, introduces you to abdominal breathing, an important step in learning to breathe to the core at will.

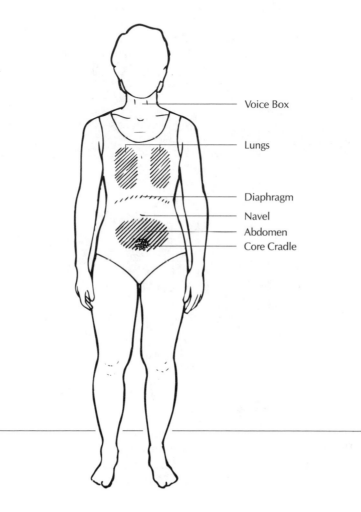

Voice Box

Lungs

Diaphragm

Navel

Abdomen

Core Cradle

FIGURE 1   Breathing Apparatus

Eyedropper

Stand erect but relaxed, being careful not to tilt or lower your head. Imagine yourself to be an upside-down eyedropper (see Figure 2). Squeeze the bulb, and air is squeezed out. Release the bulb, letting it expand, and air is drawn into the body.

Imagine that the opening tip of the glass tube ends where the back of the nose and the throat meet. Let air flow in and out through this central opening, not simply through the mouth or nose alone.

Practice applying this image as you breathe. You will find that breathing with this image in mind encourages abdominal breathing very naturally.

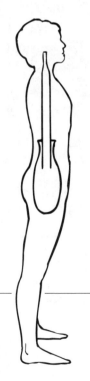

FIGURE 2   Eyedropper

Abdominal breathing does not mean that air enters into the abdomen but rather that the abdominal muscles and the sides and back of the lower torso expand outward to induce the lowering of the diaphragm, thus creating the appearance of an inflated abdomen.

The diaphragm is the main muscle used in breathing (see Figure 1); when it lowers, air is drawn into the lungs. On inhalation, air travels through the nose or mouth to the lungs, passing through the windpipe, which divides into two main bronchial tubes, one going into each lung. Oxygen in the inhaled air is transferred by the lungs to the blood, to be carried to the body tissues. Carbon dioxide, which is formed in this process, is carried by the blood back to the lungs and exhaled.

A simple inhalation of air containing oxygen cannot produce the phenomenal volume, extended range of pitches, and varied sounds and color that are demanded of a singer, nor the force and coordination demanded in the *grand jeté* of a classical dancer. The compounded energy that is developed in the body of the singer or dancer is comparable to the inner energy produced in *chi kung* to attain physical and mental well-being. The former focuses this current of energy outward, whereas the latter circulates it internally.

To further understand abdominal breathing, practice creating the mental image described in the following drill.

IMAGERY DRILL

Accordion

Create the mental image of the diaphragm as a ceiling resting on the abdominal walls (see Figure 3). Imagine that these walls and the ceiling are made of rubber that can be flexed and expanded.

From another perspective, the diaphragm is also a floor on which the lungs rest. Imagine the lungs to be a vertically held accordion. When the diaphragm drops, the accordion elongates, creating a vacuum space that sucks in air.

The whole breathing process can be summarized in this way: Expand your abdomen by curving the downstairs walls outward, causing the downstairs ceiling to lower and the upstairs floor to drop, thereby creating more space on top into which air can flow.

This image will help you to perceive how the abdomen, the lungs, and your exhalations/inhalations interact. In this drill, air is drawn in easily to fill the entire lung, and we have the illusion of air being drawn into the abdomen. In spite of its seeming simplicity, this drill demands the coordination of a juggling act. A central pivot point of control is necessary, and that is the core.

Once you are familiar with the existence and location of the core, you can stimulate it regularly and frequently with proper deep breathing. When the core is energized, all of your mental and physical performances will improve. This improvement comes not merely from being sufficiently energized but also from being able to relax unwanted muscular tension. The core works as a hub with spokes reaching out to the extremities, and the entire body can be saturated with its vibrant energy. Stress and tension can be transferred down those spokes to the core, where they can be converted into useful energy.

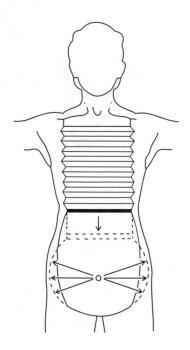

FIGURE 3 Accordian

Now practice the following imagery drills to help you get in touch with the core energy.

Funnel-Balloon

Think of the very back of your nose, where it meets the throat, as the top of a funnel. As you begin an inhalation, imagine the air you breathe as water being poured into this funnel, which leads all the way down to the end of a very long tube.

Imagine a balloon attached to the end of this tube. As you inhale easily and steadily, picture water draining down, and imagine the balloon slowly inflating. Be careful not to overfill and burst the balloon. Stop when it is comfortably full. Hold the inhaled air in the balloon for a second or so, enjoying and dwelling on that pleasant fullness. Now prepare for exhalation.

As you gradually exhale, imagine the full balloon deflating slowly, being careful to let the balloon sit firmly in place until the very end of the exhalation. After several repetitions of this exhalation/ inhalation process, you will feel warmth saturating your lower abdomen. You might even feel a throbbing or tingling sensation in other parts of your body, such as the area between your cheeks and the upper gum in your mouth, at the base of your neck, at your rib cage, and even at your kneecaps or fingertips.

Tumbling Pebble

To stimulate the sensation of activated inner energy in the lower abdomen, imagine a pebble about 1/2 inch in diameter at the center of your lower abdomen. Imagine it tumbling by its own power, over and over, slowly at first, then steadily, about one turn per second.

When you are comfortable with that sensation, you may imagine adding more pebbles to the original one, each turning and tumbling by its own power.

Eventually, with practice of these and later imagery drills, you will be mentally able to stimulate the sensation of activated inner energy. This mental stimulation is vital in order to attain the maximum benefits from your study of *chi yi*.

The Benefits of Chi Yi

Breathing is a natural reflex. So why fuss about it? If we breathe normally, some say, that's good enough. If we follow this line of thinking, we might also ask: If we can stand on our feet, why practice dancing on tiptoe? Why develop any special techniques and abilities if we are meant only to do things easily and naturally? Human beings have developed thousands of exceptional abilities and talents. We develop ourselves in order to be more functional, more wholesome, and more effective.

Among its many benefits, the technique of *chi yi* brings to its practitioners:

☐ The ability to generate inner energy.

☐ The ability to channel this inner energy selectively.

☐ The ability to respond wisely to mental and physical needs.

The core's potential is limitless. The power that comes from core development through *chi yi* will influence every aspect of your daily life—mental and physical health, energy level, personality, voice, coordination, deportment, and many other interrelated activities and characteristics. Through *chi yi*, shyness and timidity can gradually diminish, permitting your full personality to emerge. Your mental and physical movements will find a common center of gravity, and the resulting coordination produces poise, grace, and ease.

In Parts Three and Four of the book you will learn that *chi yi* has practical applications in relaxation, revitalization, improving your health, reducing or eliminating stress, tension, or pain anywhere in the body, combating insomnia, developing your athletic prowess, and much more. For now, the following section gives a preview of the benefits you may expect.

Building Confidence and Enhancing Personal Presence

In this society of keen competition and the pursuit of excellence, a person must have that extra something in order to succeed. Especially in the fields of artistic and athletic performance, a fully functioning core gives you just that—an extra, indefinable *something*.

You will learn to incorporate an awareness of your core into every sound, motion, and emotion you express: breathing, speaking, smiling, walking, running, waving, and so on. From your inner depth you will exude sincerity, conviction, and strength. From the simplest to the most complex undertaking, you will benefit from this inner support. For example, the simple motion of lifting a teacup, when performed with an awareness of and coordination extending from the core, will be noticeably more steady, graceful, and spontaneous. Similarly, a deep breath flowing from your innermost center to your face will bring a luminous, captivating glow to your complexion.

In any stage performance, alone or in collaboration with others, a successful performer, in addition to possessing talent and mastery of the required skill, must exude a captivating force that propels his or her presence into the audience. This force, often called *stage presence*, is useful to performers and public figures—and to you when you wish to command attention and project an impressive self-image. An effective core can supply this force.

Increasing Stamina, Zest, and Coordination

If you are active in a sport—whether it's tennis, swimming, figure skating, jogging, or aerobic exercise—proper deep breathing can conspicuously improve your performance. With an awareness of the core and the use of its energy, your muscles and nervous system will become more responsive, controlled, and coordinated. This awareness enhances the execution of intricate, exacting movements. You will also be able to channel your energy more effectively, resulting in increased stamina and a higher tolerance for physical exertion.

By visualizing the location of your core, you establish a focal point from which to direct your movements. Imagine that all your limbs are connected to the core, and that all your movements extend from the core. You will quickly recognize the greater sense of coordination this visualization creates, even in a simple movement such as a jumping jack.

Exhalation channels the core's energy into the execution of energetic movements. This is one of the reasons that karate students are taught to emit vocal outbursts when attacking. Some tennis players such as John McEnroe, Chris Evert, and Jimmy Connors frequently grunt with their most powerful hits—a verbal response as they use the inner energy tapped from exhalation.

As you work with the exercises, applications, and drills in this book, you will discover some breathing approaches that are particularly effective for you. Practice a few of these before you engage in your favorite sport. Work on breathing deeply and developing core energy, and see what a difference they make to your performance.

Improving the Complexion

Chi yi stimulates the flow of inner energy, bringing a vibrant glow to the surface of the skin. During the process of stimulating the core with deep breathing, the abdominal muscles flex, knead, and squeeze the organs of the abdomen, producing a massaging effect. This motion, together with activated inner energy, stimulates digestion and helps to relieve uncomfortable internal air bubbles and gas, promoting a clearer, brighter complexion. In addition, the nerve-calming effect of deep breathing will help to control the tension that is so frequently the primary cause of a bad complexion.

Freshening the Breath

Bad breath (halitosis), the kind that persists even though all hygienic precautions and proper eating habits are followed, can be helped through *chi yi* in several ways. Bad breath caused by an acidic stomach resulting from tension can be eased by relaxation through breathing. Bad breath resulting from indigestion may be eliminated through the abdominal stimulation brought on by deep breathing and inner energy. Bad breath caused by shallow breathing that traps stagnant air in the lungs can easily be remedied with a replenishing deep breathing technique.

Preparing for Childbirth

If you are an expectant father who is also a practitioner of *chi* yi, you will be able to calm your own tensions over the next nine months with deep breathing, and you will be well prepared to assist in the delivery of your child by guiding the breathing of the mother.

If you are an expectant mother who has already learned the techniques of *chi yi*, your abdominal muscles are strong and healthy—elastic and responsive. Your breathing is efficient and easy to manipulate. You are sure to benefit from these assets during your pregnancy. These qualities are also a great advantage during the delivery, when your baby—and your doctor— will need all the physical cooperation you can give. Not only will your ability to breathe effectively keep you healthier mentally and emotionally during pregnancy, your baby will benefit from your inner energy too.

If you are planning to use the Psychoprophylactic Method, a psychological and physical preparation for childbirth known also as the Lamaze Method, or any other method of natural childbirth, you will find that your ability in *chi yi is* extremely helpful in learning and carrying out these techniques. All such methods require you to train your breathing to suit the stages of delivery—dilation, transition, and expulsion. With *chi yi*, you are already expert in the control of exhalations and inhalations and in maneuvering their rate, duration, and intensity.

During the prenatal and postpartum periods, numerous physical exercises will probably be prescribed for you to help with your delivery and recovery. Explicit breathing instructions are seldom supplied with these exercises. If you already practice disciplined deep breathing, your ability to incorporate effective breathing into the exercises will greatly increase their beneficial results.

If you have never practiced *chi yi* before, you should consult your doctor before beginning these exercises during pregnancy. Every woman's physical condition varies, and every pregnancy has its own characteristics. For most normal pregnancies, the practice of *chi yi* should be helpful, whether you are a beginner or an experienced practitioner. Moderation must be observed, and your doctor's advice must always take priority. Even through the later part of your pregnancy, your doctor will most likely not object to your continuing with *chi yi*. As with swimming, tennis, and other forms of physical exercise and training, if you have been accustomed to doing it all along, there should be no harm in its continuance during a normal pregnancy.

Madame Ernestine Schumann-Heink, a famed contralto of the late nineteenth and early twentieth centuries, had many children. She was almost constantly pregnant during the prime of her career, and if she had stopped singing during her pregnancies, she would have had no career at all. Her biographers say that she performed almost up to the week of delivery and was back on stage again a few weeks after, breastfeeding her babies backstage between acts. Her breathing practice as a singer must surely have prepared her for such a devoted approach to child rearing.

Relieving Aches, Pains, and Discomforts

Aches and pains and other discomforts can arise for numerous reasons, and you should consult your physician about them if they are serious. However, if the doctor simply prescribes temporary relief such as painkillers, tranquilizers, or decongestants, you can supplement these medications with the inner energy cultivated from the practice of *chi yi*. Pains due to tension, rheumatic and arthritic pains, and lower back pain may be eliminated or greatly eased by channeling core energy to soothe the painful area.

Hastening Convalescence

For those who are convalescing or receiving physical therapy, *chi yi* can offer assistance.

An elderly friend of mine had been hospitalized for several weeks. At home again, she told me that the doctor had ordered her to get out of bed and start moving around, but she could not. She felt too weak even to sit up. I suggested that she should get up while I was visiting, first taking a few deep breaths to muster up some energy. She insisted that she could barely breathe, let alone breathe deeply. I pressed my palm firmly over her lower abdomen. As intended, my palm pressure felt heavy to her, and her abdominal muscle pushed slightly against my hand. If she could resist my palm pressure once, I told her, she could do the same a few more times with more strength.

As she did so, I asked her to synchronize her abdominal movements with her inhalation. "This is abdominal deep breathing," I told her, and she was amazed and encouraged by her accomplishment.

After she had relaxed awhile, I again called her attention to her breathing. This time I pressed against her abdomen with only my middle finger. Then I suggested that she should get up. I asked her to imagine the sensation of my finger pressing continuously against her abdomen: She could focus on that spot and from it draw all the energy she needed to stand up. With a minimum of help from her nurse, she sat up in bed, lifted her feet, and placed them on the floor. Our first goal was accomplished when she stood up by herself and slowly took a few steps to her easy chair. Her rapid recovery from then on amazed not only herself but her doctor as well, as she continued to practice this *chi yi* technique.

Certain *chi yi* exercises can be modified to fit the requirements of convalescence or disability. If you are recovering from a leg injury and are unable to stand, for example, you can execute the standing exercises and applications in this book in a sitting position. If part of your body is in a cast and cannot be moved or bent, you can still practice your breathing by eliminating the impossible motions and striking the postures indicated in the exercise or application as nearly as you can. Sensibly modified exercises and applications are still effective. Most people under physical restraint will pamper the injured area by keeping it immobile. In restricting movement, they also are likely, unconsciously, to restrain their breathing, causing it to be shallow. This limited intake of air reduces stimulation to the core and cuts down the supply of inner energy that is so necessary for recovery and healing.

Minimizing the Effects of Aging

Many people at an advanced age are suddenly confronted with the fact that their health and their very existence could have been greatly enhanced if they had put their lungs to fuller use. Shortness of breath, tight aching chest muscles, an uninspiring voice, tension, the heaving of shoulders in a useless effort to overcome the insufficient inhalation of air—all of these problems are frequently caused by poor breathing habits.

Aging is an unavoidable process characterized by the gradual loss of strength, energy, and coordination. The effects of such physical degeneration can be retarded or minimized through the development and use of core energy. Instead of fumbling aimlessly for the strength to lift yourself up, move, or walk, seek that needed strength at your core. The next time you feel too tired to stand up from sitting or stooping, visualize inward, take a deep breath, and lift up from your core as you stand. You will discover how effortless that movement can be.

Much of the image of aging is reflected in one's movement and carriage. To be able to stand more erect and to move more briskly will help you to look and feel younger.

Inner energy in a person can be likened to the electric current in a battery. When you are young, you are more fully charged, and as you proceed in life, unless you know how to recharge your inner battery, your inner energy circulation decreases steadily. When the inner energy loses some of its power and is no longer functioning at full capacity, the current will gradually withdraw, first from the farthest extremities, such as fingers, hands, and feet, and then from the arms and legs.

The joints, like the elbows in plumbing where clogging tends to occur, will also suffer from this insufficient supply of inner energy. As you grow older, you are likely to be plagued with aches and pains in these extremities—painful knuckles, aching feet, tennis elbow, and charley horses, to name a few. Any part of your body may be deprived of a sufficient supply of this inner current, leaving you unable to ward off or overcome invading illnesses.

If, when you are young and healthy, you have the foresight to develop and practice the skill of regularly generating inner energy, you will avoid the rapid decline of your inner energy stockpile. For the young of today, who frequently burn their candles at both ends, it is especially important to ensure that the supply of inner energy is not depleted but is replaced steadily. For those who are not so young, too, the supply of inner energy can be rapidly replenished and its circulation restored.

Improving Speech and Voice

No other human activity is more influenced by breathing than vocalization. Proper breathing, supported by a healthy core, will ease tension in the vocal apparatus, which is the usual cause of raspiness, hoarseness, squeakiness, breathiness, breathlessness, weakness, nasality, and many other impediments to clear speech. To mend and strengthen a misused, ailing, or underdeveloped voice, you must begin by making sure that the air you take in is correctly inhaled, energized, and exhaled.

Singing, especially classical singing, is a much more intense and demanding form of vocalization than is speech. It is an exaggerated form of elongated speech with built-in self-amplification and with extended range. In addition to musical intelligence and talent, a proficient singer needs extensive and intensive training and practice to master such intricate vocal execution. The singer must above all acquire the important technique of breath support.

When breath support is insufficient for a desired volume, inflection, or tone, whether in singing or in speech, we automatically supplement the missing energy by tensing up the chest, shoulder, or neck muscles, or all of them. But using rigid vocal cords can damage them, leading to functional problems such as soreness, breathiness, raspiness, hoarseness, loss of voice, and even the developing of nodes.

Breath is the foundation on which the voice is built, and it is only sensible to develop a reliable breathing skill, a skill that will provide sufficient energy and control for vocal support.

The image our speaking voice creates is just as important as our physical appearance. Our character, personality, state of mind, and degree of charisma are judged by how we sound. It is also true that how one sounds is related to how one looks.

Energetic, expressive speech generates obvious excitement in the listener, but a raspy, breathless, tired voice can blemish the most attractive appearance. Correct breathing is an essential component of good speech. With the help of deep breathing, a damaged voice can usually be mended. Speech defects can be smoothed out. The tone, the color, the ease, the contour of a voice can be developed. An average voice can be improved. A good voice can become more polished and perfected.

The voice possesses the unique power to express emotions through the laws of exclamatory vowels that are common to all human beings. Although the meanings of "ah," "oh," and "ee" may vary from culture to culture, their use is universal. Pitch denotes degrees of excitement. The depth of the breath relates to the depth of the vocal projection. The deeper the breath, the more thoroughly the feeling is released.

Every deep breath we take should give us a sense of wellbeing and make us feel uplifted. The world grows brighter then, and we want to open up and sing. Singing is healthy. It invites us to control a flowing stream of air and to release any pent-up emotions.

Sing anywhere you can. Sing in the shower, sing in your garden, sing in the car on the way to work. Never mind if you are tone deaf and sing out of tune. Sing for yourself. Don't worry about who may hear you. Memorize the words to a few songs—pop, rock, folk songs, hymns, even your favorite operatic arias. Don't worry if you are no Enrico Caruso or Barbra Streisand; just sing freely, comfortably. If you forget the words, make them up, or sing "la-la-la-la." Don't be shy about hearing your own voice.

Gradually, your true expressive self will emerge. You may even surprise yourself as you hear improvements in your singing. As your breathing method improves through the practice of *chi yi,* your singing voice will improve too. Let it be a barometer of your progress in learning the art of breathing.

Focusing the Breath in Meditation

Through the centuries, Buddhist monks and meditators of many faiths and beliefs have practiced meditation as a means of ascending to higher mental and spiritual plateaus; and they have asserted that the key to successful meditation is proper manipulation of the breath.

The yogis of the Himalayas went further, maintaining that controlled alternate-nostril breathing is essential. They claimed that normal breathing has a natural cycle that alternates between emphasis on the left and right nostrils. The ancient yogis believed that right-nostril breathing induced more active and aggressive instincts, while breathing through the left made one more passive and subdued. This belief brings to mind recent research on the different functions performed by the right and left hemispheres of the brain.

The practice of *chi yi* techniques establishes for you the basic ability to advance into many forms of meditation. In the process of disciplining and controlling breathing, you direct your mental attention inward, thus minimizing or even eliminating external distractions. The ability to centralize and control all mental and physical awareness is the key to total self-control of the body and mind, which is basically what meditation is all about. *Chi yi* trains the mind's eye to look inward and remain in focus, bringing about a state of total relaxation.

The ability to control your own physical and mental state produces immense satisfaction. To lie in sleeplessness or pain without the ability to combat it undermines self-confidence. Being competent in *chi yi* makes the difference between being helpless and being in charge. Begin to learn *chi yi* today!

PART TWO

Exercises for Practicing Chi Yi

Some Suggestions for Practice

What follows is the heart of *chi yi* training. These 24 exercises, arranged in six progressive lessons, guide you toward increased awareness of proper breathing habits and greater control of your breath.

Although the theory is easily grasped, diligent practice is required for the muscles and nervous system to handle this new technique reflexively. Learning *chi yi* takes motivation, concentration, and persistence. Eventually, though, taking a shallow breath will require more effort than practicing deep breathing from the abdomen. As your awareness of the breathing process is developed through the exercises, you will soon find the principles of deep breathing moving into your daily activities until you, too, are an artist in the art of breathing.

The deep-breathing skills and the resulting energy to be gained from practicing these exercises can be applied in many ways, to both physical and mental tasks. They can supplement and enhance whatever special physical skill you may be pursuing—making a business presentation, dancing, acting, or general physical activities such as jogging, aerobic exercise, or golf.

Don't be discouraged if you feel lost during your initial attempts to capture certain sensations and physical controls. With careful repetition you will begin to feel and perform as described in this book. As *chi yi* becomes habitual, you will gain in stamina, grace, radiance, and general well-being.

To some readers the exercises in this book, especially those in the first few lessons, may seem overly simple. In fact, they are very demanding because they must be performed precisely. Each detail is directed to an important purpose. The purposes of each exercise may seem abstract at first, but with practice they will soon become evident.

Each of the six lessons takes about 10 to 20 minutes to complete, depending on how much rest you require between exercises. You may decrease the number of repetitions indicated in the exercises according to your endurance. When you first begin to practice controlled breathing, you may feel slightly dizzy. Pause to recover before proceeding. Dizziness may be a signal of overexertion. Take time out for a rest interval whenever you need one, even if no rest break is indicated in the exercise instructions. If you wish to increase the number of repetitions of a particular exercise, do so with caution and with sufficient rest between repetitions.

Dress comfortably to accommodate the various movements and positions called for in the exercises. Loose comfortable clothes are recommended. Avoid constricting collars, waistbands, or belts that might restrict free and easy breathing.

The exercises do not require a lot of space, but it is a good idea to practice in a place where you can concentrate and not be interrupted. You may practice either indoors or outdoors. You will find that a stuffy room is not conducive to the practice of *chi yi*, because after the first couple of minutes of deep breathing you will begin to feel uncomfortably warm. To achieve the maximum benefit from the exercises that follow, open a window or two; it is always revitalizing to inhale fresh air.

For the exercises that are performed lying down, you will need a mat or a carpeted floor. A bare floor is not comfortable, and a soft bed does not give enough support.

You may practice any time during the day or evening, but be sure to rest at least 15 to 20 minutes after practicing before eating a meal. Also wait an hour or two after a meal before practicing, depending on how heavy a meal you have eaten.

Practice each lesson twice daily in two separate sessions. Practice each lesson for at least three days to allow sufficient time to master the skills and for your muscles to develop progressively.

After practicing a lesson twice daily for at least three consecutive days, you are ready to move on to the next lesson. If you cannot always practice twice daily, but feel thoroughly confident in performing all of the exercises in a lesson, you may proceed to the next lesson after three days. If you have skipped practicing for an entire day, it is advisable to go over each exercise once (ignoring repetitions) in the old lesson before going on to the new one. If you have not practiced for more than two days, review the previous lesson or lessons for a day or two before proceeding. In any case, let your own feeling about your mastery of the material be your guide.

Deep breathing means exhalations and inhalations that fill the upper and the lower lungs, involving the muscles of the lower torso, including the front, sides, and lower back. It is necessary to develop and tone the muscles in these areas with exercises that will induce specific results at the appropriate time. Therefore it is important to follow closely all the details specified in the exercises.

We are used to thinking of breathing as a process of inhalation-exhalation, in that order of importance. We seldom give any thought to how we exhale. Most advice on breathing emphasizes inhalation, as in "take a deep breath." The truth is that exhalation is just as important. Exhalations are cultivated and refined inner energy being selectively channeled, the reaping of what we sow when we inhale.

Important: Although the *effects* of these exercises will eventually carry over into normal breathing, the exercises themselves are intended *only* as exercises. They should not be taken as substitute methods for normal, everyday breathing. The exercises are demanding and should not be overpracticed. If signs of dizziness or other discomfort occur, stop! You have done enough for the time being. Divert your attention away from breathing by attending to other activities. Your breathing will automatically return to its normal manner and you will recuperate quickly.

Counting

In exercises where a *slow count is* indicated, each count should be executed at the rate of approximately one per second.

The numbers specified for counting mentally as we breathe are not picked arbitrarily but are chosen to gauge the duration of exhalations and inhalations under specific conditions. However, you will notice a pattern that persists throughout the book: Inhalations end with odd numbers, and exhalations end with even numbers. A psychological reason guides this usage. Most people count in pairs: At an odd number, we are mentally prepared to proceed and are therefore anticipating; at an even number we are more inclined to stop. When we end an inhalation, it is beneficial to feel anticipation and movement, whereas when we end an exhalation, it is preferable to experience a feeling of completion.

Posture

Observe the following points as you practice the exercises:

☐ Proper posture encourages proper breathing.

☐ The shoulders must never be raised or tightened. They should be relaxed and uninvolved during both exhalation and inhalation.

☐ The chest must never feel depressed or sunken.

As you sit, stand, or walk, stay erect, being careful not to stick out behind. Your head should be held straight and upright on an imaginary line drawn from the tailbone to the center top of the head. A tilted or lowered head tightens the muscles under the chin and neck, obstructing the free flow of the stream of breath.

The angle of the pelvis is essential for maintaining good posture. When you tilt your pelvis by lifting the pubic bone up in front, the abdominal and buttocks muscles are best able to support the trunk, and strain on your lower back is minimized. To further minimize straining, practice the following imagery drill.

IMAGERY DRILL

String of Beads

Imagine that your body parts are beads of different shapes. Attach a string to the floor, and string the beads. After the final bead (representing the head) is put on, pull the string taut and straight upward. All the beads should fall perfectly into place in a straight line. The different parts of your body should feel like beads on a string—well aligned, with all parts properly positioned and in place.

After a lifetime of shallow breathing, the top portion of the lungs has had more use and is stretched more than the bottom portion. We need not further emphasize the development of this top portion. On the contrary, this portion of the lungs should be left alone. Any attempt to emphasize its use will distract from and impede the development of the lower portion. Eventually, when the level of functional ability and elasticity of the lower lungs matches that of the top, both will automatically function together as a whole.

If you have ever blown up a long balloon, you will remember that balloons of this shape inflate easily only at the end where air enters. Unless you manipulate the balloon, the far end will scarcely inflate at all. You may have noticed that after several tries the inflated end becomes much looser and more elastic than the other end, creating an even greater tendency toward one-ended inflation. One trick to overcome this situation is to stretch and pull the far end of the balloon manually, loosening up the far end before inflating it.

The lungs are like this long balloon. Due to a variety of physical circumstances the bottom part of the lungs, like the far end of the balloon, is hardly used. Unless we do something about shallow breathing, the lungs will become increasingly top-heavy as we grow older. The progressive exercises in this book will deter this unhealthy condition. You will frequently hear elderly— and sometimes not so elderly—people complaining about the difficulty of breathing. Often this condition arises as the top part of the lungs becomes overburdened and overused and loses its elasticity, while the lower part of the lungs is undeveloped and incapable of undertaking its share of the lungs' function. It is never too late to begin training your lower lungs to be functional through the practice of *chi yi*.

Developing Internal Sensations and Muscular Controls

As you practice each of the exercises in the upcoming six lessons, try to maintain your awareness of the following sensations and means of muscular control. *Refer frequently to these two lists to increase your awareness of these qualities.*

Internal Sensations

☐ Be conscious of the *lower abdominal area,* located below the navel, which is inflatable and deflatable.

☐ Experience the sensation of breath flowing into and inflating the *lower abdomen* during inhalation.

☐ Experience the sensation of the deflation of the *lower abdomen* during exhalation.

☐ Experience a mental image and the sensation of the *tongue* extending from the tip to its root, not ending at the throat or the neck or the chest but extending all the way down to the pit of the stomach.

☐ As the tip of the *tongue* touches the back of the top front teeth during inhalation, imagine the tongue as a conduit. Air travels along this conduit from the nostrils past the tip of the tongue and flows all the way down to the tongue's root. At this point the stream of air loops around and travels back up and out.

☐ Experience the sensation of the *tongue's* relaxed positions. The tongue should feel limp and relaxed, not a tight lump or an inflexible strip. A tense tongue can cause tension in the neck, chest, and shoulder muscles, restricting the free flow of air into the lower abdomen.

☐ Experience the sensation of stimulating the *tongue's root so* that it more fully participates in the visible tongue's control and movement. Elongation, movement, and relaxation of the visible part of the tongue establishes sensation in the root and reinforces your ability to relocate tongue tension to the core as you breathe abdominally.

☐ Whenever "hold breath" is indicated between inhalation and exhalation, create a sensation of that breath continuously sinking and settling down to the bottom of the *abdomen* during the "hold" period.

☐ During exhalation, create a sensation of air being drained through a hole in the bottom of the *abdomen*.

☐ Experience the yawning sensation (at the *back of the throat* and the adjoining *nasal passage*) that creates a central opening for the flow of air.

Muscular Controls

☐ To obtain proper opening of the mouth for exercise, stretch the jaws open not only in front but all the way back to the jaw hinges so that the top and bottom molars form an almost parallel line. You can attain it only if the *jaws* are opened in a rounded "reclining U" shape (⊃), not in an angular "reclining V" shape (>).

☐ Breathe freely as you practice the exercises that emphasize your *neck muscles*.

☐ Produce a *steady stream of breath* instead of disjointed short puffs.

☐ Initiate movements of the arms, legs, spine, neck, and so on by inner energy from the *lower abdomen*.

☐ Strengthen the *lower abdominal muscles* by expanding outward and pulling inward at will, with or without breathing.

☐ Use your fingertips and palms to assist and monitor the movements of the *abdominal muscles* whenever necessary.

Leading the Breath

Lesson 1 introduces a natural, simple, and effective method of breath discipline. The four exercises in Lesson 1 are designed to stretch your abdominal and lower back torso muscles. These muscles are among the principal elements involved in the kind of deep breathing that comes so naturally to healthy infants and is often lost as we grow older.

Through neglect and lack of exercise, the muscles of the abdominal wall and the lower back torso become rigid and unresponsive. Another factor in the avoidance of diaphragmatic deep breathing is the cultural attitude that regards protrusion of the abdomen as unfashionable. These and other properly designed breathing exercises do not make the stomach muscles protrude. On the contrary, development of these muscles reduces flabbiness, adds strength and elasticity, and increases your ability to hold your stomach in when you desire to do so.

Lesson 1 also helps you to develop your awareness of the yawning sensation at the back of the nose and throat that you achieve when inhaling. This sensation, which is emphasized in the Eyedropper Imagery Drill, induces the nose-throat junction to act as a wide funnel for the deep, free flow of air.

Once you are familiar with the exercises, the first lesson can be completed in 5 to 10 minutes, but be careful not to rush the exercises, or to skip any steps. This first lesson introduces movements and sensations that are essential to the lessons that follow. Practice it carefully twice a day for at least three days, until you feel comfortable with all the exercises.

EXERCISE 1A

Stretching the Abdominal Muscles

In a sitting position, all muscles, especially those of the legs, are more relaxed. In this position you can readily focus your attention on the abdominal muscles.

Sitting straight is important in order to form a right angle at the torso-buttocks junction. This position gives the lower abdominal area a maximum spread upward, which in turn allows greater breath capacity.

1. Sit up straight in a chair with your feet on the floor 6 to 7 inches apart.

2. Place your hands against the lower abdominal wall with your palms inward, fingertips not quite meeting (see Figure 4).

FIGURE 4

3. Place the tip of your tongue behind your bottom front teeth. Exhale through your mouth by blowing gently through slightly pursed lips to a slow count of 1-2-3-4-5. Begin the exhalation from the abdomen, simultaneously deflating the abdominal wall and adding inward pressure from the fingertips. On the sixth count, exert extra pressure to deflate the abdomen completely.

4. Place the tip of your tongue against the back of your top front teeth. Inhale through your nose as you create a yawning sensation in the back of the nose and throat to a slow count of 1-2-3-4-5-6. At the same time, expand the lower abdominal wall outward. On the seventh count, give the lower abdominal wall an extra push outward with an emphatic intake of breath to reach maximum expansion.

5. Without pausing, repeat the exhale-inhale sequence (steps 3 and 4) three times.

6. If you have never attempted to control your breathing before, you may feel slightly dizzy at this time. Don't be alarmed. Just relax for a few minutes before going on to the next exercise.

EXERCISE 1B

Stretching the Lower Back Muscles

When you bend over from a sitting position, the lower back muscles are stretched to their maximum length, and air can easily be inhaled to that area.

Holding your hands on your ankles with your elbows turned outward further encourages the spreading and extending of the lower back torso.

It is important to sit with your feet 10 to 12 inches apart. If the feet are too close together, the lower front abdominal muscle is restricted; if they are too far apart, the tailbone tends to stick out, resulting in a swayback that restricts the lower back muscles.

1. Sit up straight in a chair with your feet on the floor 10 to 12 inches apart. Place your hands in your lap, palms downward. Turn your palms inward with your thumbs toward your body, allowing your elbows to turn outward and forward. Gently grasp your upper thighs with your thumbs on the outside and your fingers on the inside of your thighs (see Figure 5).

2. Bend forward gradually while sliding your hands down your legs toward your ankles (see Figure 6). Firmly grasp the ankles (or the legs as close to the ankles as comfortably possible). Bend your head downward toward the floor, and turn your elbows farther out. In this position, focus your attention on your lower back and tailbone.

3. With your head still down, place the tip of your tongue behind your bottom front teeth. Exhale through your mouth by blowing gently through slightly pursed lips to a slow count of 1-2-3-4. At the same time, gradually deflate the lower abdominal wall.

4. Hold your breath, and remain still for a moment.

5. Place the tip of your tongue against the back of your top front teeth. Inhale through your nose, creating a yawning

sensation at the back of the nose and throat, to a slow count of 1-2-3-4-5. Direct the air you are inhaling toward the base of your torso. Imagine elongating the spine as you inhale while inflating the lower back torso. On the fifth count, give both sides of the lower back torso an extra expansion outward with an emphatic intake of breath.

6. Hold your breath, as you slowly sit up, sliding your hand back onto your lap.

7. Exhale completely.

8. Repeat steps 1 through 7 four times.

9. Relax for a few minutes before going on to Exercise 3.

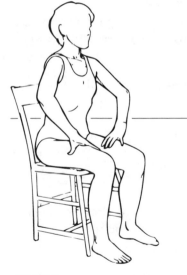

FIGURE 5

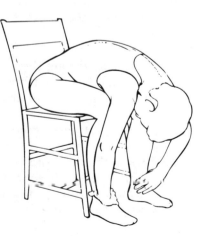

FIGURE 6

EXERCISE 1C

Stretching the Muscles at the Base of the Torso

Spreading the knees as far apart as possible in a kneeling position expands the lower torso. This posture draws your attention to the lower abdominal muscles and focuses muscular activity at the point where inflating and deflating most effectively take place.

Sliding your hands downward while inhaling deters your shoulders from heaving and discourages air from flowing uncontrollably and exclusively into the upper torso. The aim of this movement is to fill the lower torso with breath first, and then gradually let the breath pile upward. The feeling of fullness of breath must progress from bottom to top without allowing the lower area to deflate.

1. Kneel with your back and upper legs straight and at a right angle to your lower legs, and with your toes pointing to the back.

2. Spread your knees as far apart as possible without bending your body.

3. Place your hands just above the hips with palms inward, fingers pointing downward, and thumbs forward. Spread your elbows to the sides (see Figure 7).

4. Place the tip of your tongue against your bottom front teeth. Exhale through your mouth by blowing gently through slightly pursed lips to a slow count of 1-2-3-4-5-6 while deflating the lower abdomen.

5. Place the tip of your tongue against your top front teeth. Inhale through your nose, creating a yawning sensation at the back of the nose and throat, to a slow count of 1-2-3-4-5-6-7. Simultaneously inflate the lower abdomen and slide your hands gradually down your thighs until your arms are straight (see Figure 8).

6. Place the tip of your tongue against your bottom front teeth. Exhale through your mouth to a slow count of 1-2-3-4-5-6 while pulling your hands gradually back up to their original upper-hip-level position and deflating the lower abdomen.

7. Repeat steps 5 and 6 three times.

8. Remain in position and breathe freely.

9. Relax for a few minutes before going on to Exercise 4.

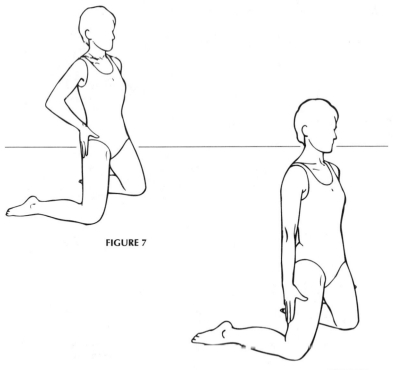

FIGURE 7

FIGURE 8

Stretching the Lower Front and Back Torso

The standing position does not induce the stretching or flexing of your torso muscles. In this neutral position, a higher degree of mental control of abdominal and lower back muscles is required to achieve the desired physical effect.

Joining hands behind your back and pushing them downward prevents your shoulders from heaving as you extend the front torso. Bending down while exhaling assists the contraction of the lower front abdominal muscles. Then, as you return to the standing position while inhaling, the inhaled air flows easily into the lower front abdominal area.

1. Stand up straight with your feet 18 to 20 inches apart.

2. Hold your head up straight; do not lower your chin (see Figure 9).

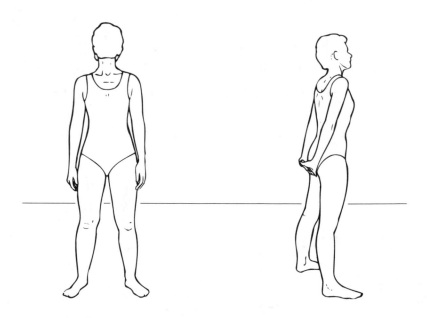

FIGURE 9   **FIGURE 10**

3. Join your hands together behind your back, palms down, locking your fingers.

4. Stretch your locked hands downward as far as possible, being careful not to stick your tailbone out and backward (see Figure 10).

5. Place the tip of your tongue against your bottom front teeth. Exhale through your mouth by blowing gently through slightly pursed lips to a slow count of 1-2-3-4-5-6 while gradually bending forward as far as possible and deflating the lower abdominal wall (see Figure 11).

6. Place the tip of your tongue against your top front teeth. Inhale through your nose, creating a yawning sensation at the back of your nose and throat, to a slow count of 1-2-3-4-5-6-7 while expanding the lower abdominal wall and lower back, returning to the original standing position described in steps 1 through 4.

7. Repeat steps 5 and 6 five times.

8. Exhale, relax, and rest.

FIGURE 11

Thoughts on Lesson 1

The points made in Lesson 1 are simple, yet frequently the most obvious point may prove to be the one most easily overlooked. The most instinctive act, such as walking, frequently turns out to be difficult or even distorted.

Besides the objectives already discussed in Exercises 1A through 1D of Lesson 1, two very basic mental points must be introduced and established.

First, always think of the breath sequence as exhalation/ inhalation instead of the reverse. At any relaxed instant, some air always remains in the lungs; by expelling this leftover air, you are ready to start your first conscious inhalation afresh.

Second, the outflowing and inflowing of air (exhalation and inhalation) should produce no audible sounds. The sounds of gasping can be very disruptive, and even annoying, especially in speakers, singers, and wind instrumentalists. The split seconds that are allowed for air intake between phrases of speech or music demand that you leave your nose and mouth openings unobstructed. If you think about drawing in air through these openings, the muscles in these areas will be tense and narrow. Instead, apply the mental picture described in the Eyedropper Imagery Drill. Let the air be drawn in by your lower abdomen (the rubber bulb, as you imagine it), simultaneously letting your nose-throat junction act as a passive receptacle, like the top of a funnel. The muscles in these openings will then be relaxed and stretchable, allowing air to flow freely and silently.

LESSON 2

Coordinating the Breath

When your tongue is tense and pulled in an inflexible lump toward the back of the throat, it obstructs the free flow of the breath and impairs your speech. Tension in the tongue extends to the throat, shoulder, chest, and abdominal muscles, preventing inhaled air from flowing freely to the bottom of the lungs. The relaxed tongue is crucial to deep breathing.

A continuous muscular connection runs from the tip of the tongue to the pit of the stomach. By learning to relax the tip of the tongue, and to mentally relocate its tension to the core, you will learn to relieve the tension of the tongue and to stimulate the core as well.

Open your mouth wide when doing the tongue exercises in this lesson to give maximum room for free movement of the tongue and the breath. A very small proportion of people may have weak jaw hinge muscles, so be careful not to strain these muscles by performing overexaggerated jaw movements for an extended period of time. If you do strain your jaw hinges, gentle massage with the fingertips will bring instant relief.

RECOMMENDED REVIEW   EXERCISES 1A, 1B, AND 1D

The review exercises can work as an integral part of the lessons. They are designed to fit into a group of exercises that are aimed at a specific purpose. As you do these exercises sequentially, you may become aware of the relationships among them. As you repeat them in the order given in the Review, you will be more aware of the cumulative nature of several exercises. The review of specific exercises, in a specific order, is also designed to strengthen your ability to perform them and to ease you into new exercises.

Review Exercises 1A, 1B, and 1D to recapture the sensations developed in Lesson 1. The specified repetitions in the review exercises can be reduced to leave you enough time and energy to complete Lesson 2.

EXERCISE 2A

Draining Tongue and Tongue Root Tension into the Core

This exercise stretches and extends the neck tendons and muscles and relieves any tension or kinks you may have.

Stretching your locked hands downward behind your back prevents your shoulders from heaving and inhibits inhaled air from flooding the upper torso and blocking the smooth flow of air into the lower abdomen.

If possible, perform Exercise 2A in front of a mirror; it is important to monitor the mouth and tongue positions closely. During this exercise, be sure you don't raise your shoulders while practicing the mouth and tongue movements. Your tongue should remain relaxed at all times.

1. Stand with your feet 10 to 12 inches apart.

2. Tilt your head back as far as possible; then bring it to an upright position in which it is tilted back slightly.

3. Join your hands together behind your back, locking your fingers.

4. Lower your locked hands to your buttocks, being careful not to stick your tailbone out and backward.

5. Open your mouth wide and touch your tongue to your top front teeth at a point about 1/2 to 3/4 inch in from the tip of your tongue (see Figure 12).

6. Inhale through your mouth to a slow count of 1-2-3-4 while inflating the lower abdomen.

7. Place the tip of your relaxed tongue behind your bottom front teeth (see Figure 13). Exhale through your mouth by blowing gently to a slow count of 1-2-3-4-5 while deflating the lower abdomen.

8. Once again, open your mouth wide and touch your tongue to your bottom front teeth at a point 1/2 to 3/4 inch in from the tip (see Figure 14).

9. Inhale through your mouth to a slow count of 1-2-3-4 while inflating the lower abdomen.

10. Place the tip of your tongue behind your bottom front teeth (see Figure 13). Exhale through your mouth to a slow count of 1-2-3-4-5 while deflating the lower abdomen.

11. Repeat steps 5 through 10 two more times.

12. Relax for a few minutes before going on to the next segment.

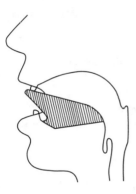

FIGURE 12

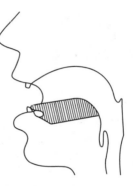

FIGURE 13

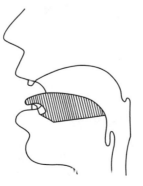

FIGURE 14

EXERCISE 2A CONTINUED

During this segment, be sure to hold your head erect; in stretching the tongue downward toward the chin, the head tends to dip, causing the under-chin and neck muscles to tighten.

When your tongue is stretched as far as possible toward your chin, as in step 5 below, be sure your mouth remains wide open.

1. Stand up straight with your feet 10 to 12 inches apart.

2. Tilt your head back as far as possible; then return it to an upright position in which it is tilted back slightly. Do not lower your chin.

3. Join your hands together behind your back, locking your fingers.

4. Lower your locked hands to your buttocks, being careful not to stick your tailbone out and backward.

5. Open your mouth wide, stretching the jawbone hinges. Stick your tongue out as far as possible toward your chin (see Figure 15).

6. Keep your mouth wide open and your tongue out. Exhale by blowing gently to a slow count of 1-2-3-4-5 while deflating the lower abdomen.

7. Maintain the mouth and tongue positions as described in steps 5 and 6. Inhale through your mouth to a slow count of 1-2-3-4 while inflating the lower abdomen.

8. Keep your mouth open, and bring your relaxed tongue behind your bottom front teeth (see Figure 16). Exhale through your mouth to a slow count of 1-2-3-4-5 while deflating the lower abdomen.

9. Maintain the mouth and tongue positions described in step 8. Inhale through your mouth to a slow count of 1-2-3-4 while inflating the lower abdomen.

10. Repeat steps 5 through 9 three times.

11. Drop your hands to your sides, loosen your joints, breathe freely, and relax for a few minutes before going on to Exercise 2B.

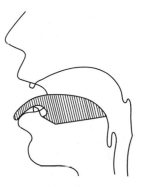

FIGURE 15

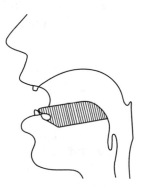

FIGURE 16

EXERCISE 2B

Activating the Tongue Muscles

In this exercise, the syllable *toh is* a nonvocal or aspirated sound, as in whispering, made merely by the quick release of breath. It sounds like *tore* without the r sound, except that it is produced without the involvement of the voice box. Air should explode out between the front teeth and the tip of the tongue to produce a nonvocal outburst.

When making a double *toh-toh* sound, you should produce two explosive snapping sounds, one after the other, using only the lower abdominal muscles and inhaling no additional breath.

IMAGERY DRILL

Cannonball

Imagine an unobstructed channel from the pit of your stomach to the tip of your tongue as you produce nonvocal *tohs. It* may also help to imagine the *tohs* as cannonballs being shot through the channel from the pit of the stomach to the tip of the tongue and beyond.

In the exercise that follows, all snapping inward (rapid deflating) must be done with the lower abdominal and lower back torso muscles only. The only upper torso and chest movements should be slight natural reactions to the abdominal movements. You should experience no upward thrusts or jerks of the shoulders, the top back torso, or the chest.

1. Sit up straight in a chair with your head facing forward. Place both feet on the floor 6 to 8 inches apart, with your toes pointing slightly outward. Place your hands against the lower abdominal wall, palms inward and fingertips almost touching.

2. Place the tip of your tongue against the back of your bottom front teeth. Exhale through your mouth by blowing gently through slightly pursed lips to a slow count of 1-2-3-4-5-6 while deflating the lower abdominal wall, using your fingertips to apply extra pressure.

3. Place the tip of your tongue firmly against your top front teeth. With your mouth closed, inhale through your nose to a slow count of 1-2-3-4-5 while inflating the lower abdominal wall.

4. Bring the tip of your tongue between your top and bottom front teeth. Release the syllable *toh* explosively, dropping your jaw as you do so (see Figure 17). Do not retract your tongue toward your throat but simply release the tip of your tongue from your front teeth while dropping your jaw. Simultaneously snap the lower abdominal wall inward, assisting with pressure from your fingertips.

5. Exhale the remaining air.

6. Repeat steps 3 through 5 four times.

7. Relax, and rest for a moment.

8. Repeat steps 3 through 6 again, substituting a double *toh-toh* sound (staccato) for *toh*.

9. Repeat step 8 six times.

10. Relax, and rest briefly.

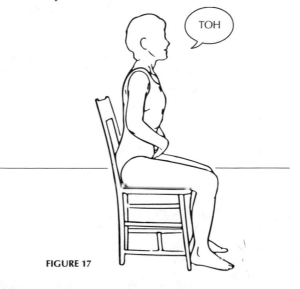

FIGURE 17

Controlling the Tip and the Root of the Tongue

The purpose of this exercise is to create awareness of core energy. The sound *tse* is a nonvocalized tight hissing sound produced by a continuous stream of breath. To make the *tse* sound, bring your top and bottom teeth together, but do not bite down hard. Place the tip of your tongue gently against the back of your front teeth. It's important for the tongue not to press too strongly against the front teeth, as extreme pressure causes tension in the neck and tongue. Exhale in an even, steady, unrushed stream of breath to produce not a *se* but a *tse* sound.

Although pressure is being produced by a continuous deflation of the lower abdominal wall, this deflation should not be overly exaggerated with too much inward motion of the abdominal wall. You can avoid this tendency by creating an imaginary counterforce from within, such as an expanding sensation within your lower abdomen as you deflate it. In this way, a much more controlled pressure of the abdominal wall can be produced and put to use.

1. Sit up straight in a chair with your head tilted back slightly. Place your feet on the floor 6 to 8 inches apart, with your toes pointing slightly outward. Place your hands against the lower abdominal wall, palms inward, fingertips almost touching.

2. Place the tip of your tongue gently against your bottom front teeth. Exhale through your mouth by blowing through slightly pursed lips to a slow count of 1-2-3-4-5-6, while squeezing in the abdominal wall with added pressure from your fingertips.

3. Place the tip of your tongue firmly against your top front teeth. Inhale through your nose to a slow count of 1-2-3-4-5, while inflating the lower abdomen.

4. Touch your top and bottom teeth together; do not bite hard. Place the tip of your tongue against the inside of your front teeth.

5. Exhale by producing a sustained *tse* sound (see Figure 18) while performing the following steps alternately:

   ☐ Roll your head in a clockwise circle once, then counter-clockwise once.

   ☐ Seesaw your shoulders up and down twice.

6. As you maintain the sustained *tse* sound, you will begin to feel a gradual tightening of a central spot in the depth of the lower abdomen. You are beginning to localize and gain an awareness of your core. Continue making the sustained *tse* sound until your breath is depleted.

7. Hold the deflated position for a few seconds. Then give an extra squeeze of the abdominal muscles, with added pressure from your fingertips, to expel any remaining air with an additional *tse*.

8. Immediately inhale deeply through your nose, with the tip of your tongue firmly against your top front teeth. Settle your breath, and hold it for a few seconds.

9. Exhale and relax for a moment. Repeat steps 2 through 8 once more.

10. Exhale, and rest briefly, and proceed to the following segment.

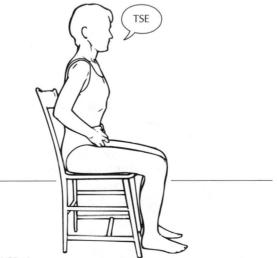

FIGURE 18

EXERCISE 2C CONTINUED

The purpose of this segment is to learn how to maintain constant control of the core while sitting, standing, walking, running, jumping, or performing other movements.

When rising from a sitting to a standing position in step 6, take care not to shift pressure away from the core, the center of the lower abdomen.

In step 7, be especially careful not to let the center point shift to the chest, shoulders, or neck. Steady fingertip pressure on the lower abdomen will help alleviate this tendency to shift.

1. Sit up straight in a chair facing a desk or table. Place your feet on the floor with your weight on your toes, as if you were about to stand up. Place one foot slightly in front of the other.

2. Place your right hand (or your left, if you are left-handed) on the table top, palm down. Place the other hand against the lower abdominal wall, palm inward.

3. Place the tip of your tongue lightly against your bottom front teeth. Exhale through your mouth by blowing through slightly pursed lips to a slow count of 1-2-3-4-5-6, while squeezing the lower abdominal muscle inward and pressing with your fingertips.

4. Place the tip of your tongue firmly against your top front teeth. Inhale deeply through your nose to a slow count of 1-2-3-4-5, while inflating the lower abdomen.

5. Bring your upper and lower teeth together, but do not bite down hard. Place the tip of your tongue gently against the back of your front teeth while maintaining the air pressure in your lower abdomen.

6. Exhale by producing the sustained *tse* sound described in Exercise 2A (see Figure 19). Simultaneously, stand up, using the hand on the table to assist balance. Do not allow your shoulders to rise or your body to bend forward.

7. When you have reached an upright position, continue the *tse* sound evenly and firmly, using your lower abdominal and lower back muscles to maintain breath support (see Figure 20).

8. When your breath is depleted, hold in that state for 2 to 3 seconds. Then blow out forcefully, deflating the abdominal wall to expel any remaining air.

9. Immediately inhale deeply through your nose with the tip of your tongue held firmly against your top front teeth. Hold your breath without straining for a few seconds.

10. Slowly and deeply exhale and inhale three times, with accompanying lower abdomen deflation and inflation.

11. Relax, and rest for a moment.

12. Repeat this exercise two more times with a rest interval between repetitions.

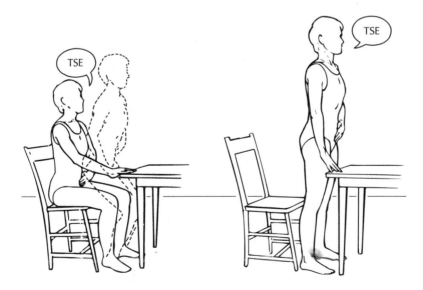

FIGURE 19   **FIGURE 20**

EXERCISE 2D

Stretching the Muscles of the Lower Torso

Raising your hands above your head stretches the torso length-wise. The previous exercises should have stretched your lower torso sideways sufficiently to enable you to maintain a stable, anchored base during this exercise.

In a left-right, backward-forward sequence of movements while inhaling and exhaling, you will learn to squeeze air out of your torso one side at a time, and then draw air back into your torso one side at a time. This action will allow you to make each repeated inhalation and exhalation more emphatic.

1. Stand up straight with your feet spread apart to the width of your shoulders. Point your toes slightly outward.

2. Raise your arms over your head and lock your fingers, palms down, to form an arch (see Figure 21).

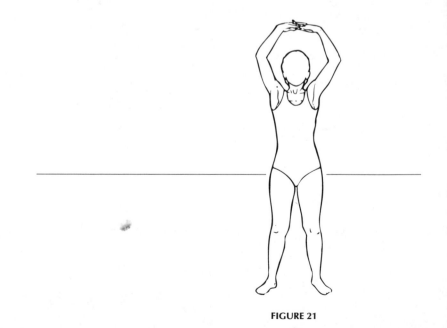

FIGURE 21

3. Place the tip of your tongue lightly against your bottom front teeth. Exhale through your mouth by blowing gently through slightly pursed lips to a slow count of 1-2-3-4-5-6-7-8. Simultaneously:

   ☐ Rock the arch from the waist, left-right-left-right on the counts 1-2-3-4, and slowly deflate the lower abdomen (see Figures 22 and 23).

   ☐ Return on counts 5 and 6 to the center upright position described in step 2.

4. Place the tip of your tongue firmly against your top front teeth. Inhale deeply through your nose to a slow count of 1-2-3-4-5-6. Simultaneously:

   ☐ Bend in an arch from the waist, moving forward to a slow count of 1-2 backward to a slow count of 3-4, and inflate the lower back and abdomen (see Figures 24 and 25).

   ☐ Return to the center upright position on count 5-6 (see Figure 21).

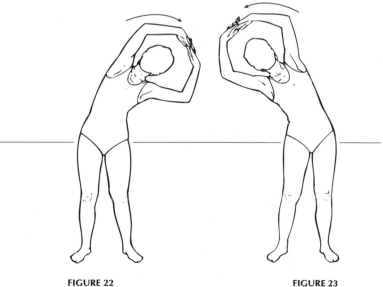

FIGURE 22   FIGURE 23

5. Repeat steps 3 and 4 four times.

6. Exhale through your mouth to a slow count of 1-2-3-4-5-6-7-8, while deflating the lower abdomen and lowering your arms to your sides.

7. Inhale, relax, and rest.

FIGURE 24　　　　　　　　　　　　**FIGURE 25**

Thoughts on Lesson 2

By this time, your muscles should be growing more sensitive and responsive, and your awareness of the core gradually becoming more acute.

Exercises 1A through 2D were geared toward maximum inflation and deflation of the abdomen. Keeping in mind the image of the body as a pyramid, you should begin to cultivate a sensation of physical stability.

You should be able to feel your core glowing with energy, generated from within.

LESSON 3

Controlling the Breath

In addition to the tongue, the neck is another part of the body that must be fully relaxed before effective breathing can take place. Without some form of abdominal breathing, however, it is difficult to relax the neck. To break this circle, you must follow a regimen that focuses alternately on developing each of these skills so that they reinforce each other.

It is not easy to get rid of unwanted tension in the neck, tongue, or shoulders. Tension in these areas must be relocated to a place where, properly handled, it can be recycled into useful energy. The core is such a place. Awareness of the core must be established before harmful tensions can be effectively eliminated. This lesson also reestablishes the relationship between the tongue and the core by reviewing Exercise 2B.

From now on, you will no longer be instructed to rest between exercises. Let your physical condition determine when you need to rest, and for how long.

The Elastic Band Imagery Drill will help you to relax your neck as well as your chest and back muscles. You will feel taller, straighter, and free of muscle tension, especially in the neck area.

IMAGERY DRILL

Elastic Band

Visualize your spine, with its ability to bend in any direction. Imagine one elastic band attached from your chin to your lower abdomen, and another attached from the back of your head (at the top) to your lower back. Bend backward, with your chin lifted high, and feel the front elastic band stretching to its utmost. Bend forward with your head dipping low and feel the back elastic band stretching as much as possible.

Imagine that these elastic bands are too stiff and tight. As you bend backward and forward you lengthen the bands and relax the stiffness and tightness.

EXERCISE 3A

Directing the Breath to the Lower Abdomen and Lower Back

Lying down should be a very relaxed position, yet many people find themselves unable to relax sufficiently to fall asleep. To do away with unwanted tension, focus your mind on the core by directing the breath there. This will create a magnetic center where tensions can be gathered and dispelled or recycled. In this exercise, tension is maintained at the core and used to bend the knees and pull the feet toward the body. Drawing the knees to the chest further emphasizes the involvement of the lower back in abdominal breathing.

1. Lie on the floor or bed with your feet together. Place your hands, palms down, on the floor by your sides, 12 to 14 inches away from the body (see Figure 26).

2. Bend your knees and slide your feet flat along the floor until they are as close to your body as possible (see Figure 27).

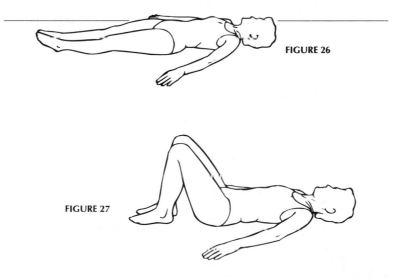

FIGURE 26

FIGURE 27

3. Place the tip of your tongue against your bottom front teeth. Exhale on the counts of 1 and 2 by blowing through your mouth in two strong gusts (one gust to each count), while deflating the lower abdomen and doing the following steps:

   ☐ With the first gust, swing your knees up as close to your chest as possible, lifting your feet off the floor (see Figure 28).

   ☐ With the second gust, return your feet to the floor (see Figure 27).

4. Place the tip of your tongue against your top front teeth. Inhale through your nose in two strong sniffs (one to each count), while inflating the lower abdomen and doing the following steps:

   ☐ With the first sniff, swing your knees up as close to your chest as possible, lifting your feet off the floor (see Figure 28).

   ☐ With the second sniff, return your feet to the floor (see Figure 27).

5. Repeat steps 3 and 4 in a rocking motion ten times.

6. Exhale as you straighten your legs, and return to your original position.

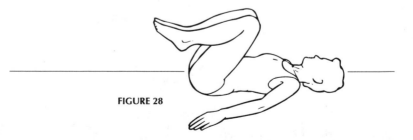

FIGURE 28

EXERCISE 3B

Relieving Neck Tension

This exercise is intended to stretch the spine, back muscles, and tendons at the same time that breathing is being controlled. When you hook your arms under your knees, as in step 3, you stretch the back and side muscles outward and keep your shoulders from heaving. Bending your head and touching your face to your knees extends your back and the back of your neck lengthwise.

In the ball position, with your stomach curled inside, exhaling further shrinks the front abdominal wall. In this position, the back is extended and the front is contracted as much as possible. This position also directs the maximum amount of breath to the lower back while restricting intake to the front. Extreme positions such as this one help you develop agility.

1. Sit up straight on the floor and stretch your legs out in front of you. Place your feet together and point your toes, making sure you are sitting up straight. Hold your head in an upright position, being careful not to drop your chin. Place your hands on your knees, palms down (see Figure 29).

2. Slide your feet toward you, bending your knees (see Figure 30).

FIGURE 29   **FIGURE 30**

3. Hook your arms under your knees by reaching under the knees with your right hand to hold your left elbow or near to it, and with your left hand to hold your right elbow or near to it (see Figure 31).

4. Bend your head over and touch your face to your knees, or as close as you can comfortably manage (see Figure 32).

5. Place the tip of your tongue against your bottom front teeth. Exhale through your mouth by blowing gently through slightly pursed lips to a slow count of 1-2-3-4-5-6, while completely deflating the lower abdomen.

6. Hold your breath and remain still for a second.

7. Place the tip of your tongue against your top front teeth. Inhale through your nose to a slow count of 1-2-3-4-5-6-7, while inflating the lower abdomen. As you inhale, think of your lower torso as a round balloon that inflates as you inhale steadily to the count of 1-2-3-4-5. On the last two counts, make an extra effort to fully inflate the balloon, using your lower back and side muscles.

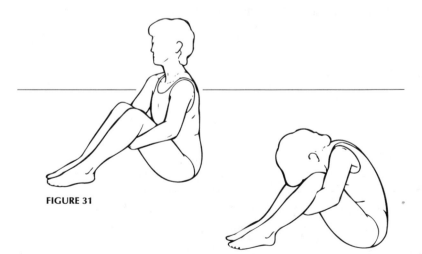

FIGURE 31

FIGURE 32

Sitting up straight with your feet as far apart as possible focuses attention on the lower abdominal area, the core's cradle. Bending your knees with your feet far apart makes you more fully aware of the lower back. Placing your hands on your knees helps you maintain your balance, and lowers and relaxes the shoulders and upper chest muscles as well. Be sure that your shoulders remain relaxed as you bend your knees and shift your hands from knees to ankles.

By rolling your head in a dangling, relaxed position, you ensure that the neck is completely relaxed while the lower torso is energetically controlling the breathing.

RECOMMENDED REVIEW   EXERCISES 1B AND 2B

For the exercises in this lesson, you must be very aware of the relationship between your tongue and the act of breathing to and from the core. Reread the introductory material for Lesson 2 before reviewing Exercise 2B.

A review of Exercise 1B gives you the opportunity to loosen the lower torso and establish a firmer focus on your core. This exercise will also loosen the muscles and tendons at the back of the neck in preparation for Exercise 3C.

EXERCISE 3C

Relieving Neck and Shoulder Tension

Swinging your arms relaxes your shoulders and loosens the base of the neck. Your arms should dangle and swing freely. It is preferable to keep your elbow joints loose by letting your elbows bend slightly, as is their natural tendency.

Your neck muscles should not be tense during the alternating neck stretches. Relax!

1. Stand up straight with your feet 12 to 14 inches apart and your toes pointed slightly outward.

2. Lower your shoulders, and loosen your shoulder joints. Let your arms and hands dangle at your sides (see Figure 36). Stretch and extend your neck upward.

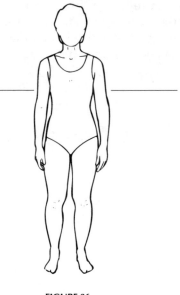

FIGURE 36

3. Place the tip of your tongue against your bottom front teeth. Gently tilt your head back as far as possible to stretch the front of your neck and stretch all the way to the core. Exhale through your mouth by blowing vigorously through slightly pursed lips to a slow count of 1-2, while deflating the lower abdomen and doing the following:

   ☐ On the first count, swing your arms to the left, bringing your hands toward waist level (see Figure 37).

   ☐ On the second count, swing your arms to the right, bringing your hands toward waist level (see Figure 38).

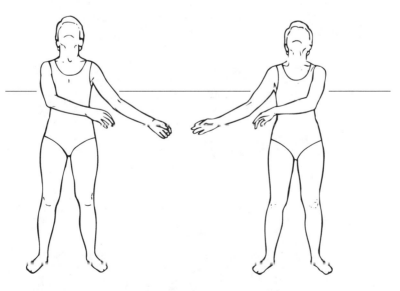

FIGURE 37   FIGURE 38

4. Place the tip of your tongue against your top front teeth. Bend your head forward as far as possible to stretch the back of your neck. Inhale vigorously through your nose to a slow count of 1-2, while inflating the lower abdomen and doing the following:

   □ On the first count, swing your arms to the left, bringing your hands toward waist level (see Figure 39).

   □ On the second count, swing your arms to the right, bringing your hands toward waist level (see Figure 40).

5. Repeat steps 3 and 4 seven times.

6. Return to upright standing position.

7. Relax momentarily and proceed to the following segment.

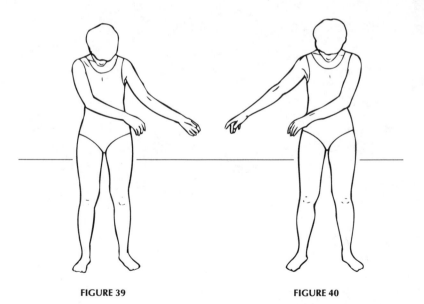

FIGURE 39   **FIGURE 40**

EXERCISE 3C CONTINUED

Swinging your arms forward and backward as suggested in this segment further relaxes the front and back of the rib cage.

1. Stand up straight with your feet 10 to 12 inches apart and your toes turned slightly outward.

2. Lower your shoulders, and loosen your shoulder joints. Let your arms and hands dangle at your sides. Stretch and extend your neck.

3. Place the tip of your tongue against your bottom front teeth. Tilt your head back as far as possible to stretch the front of your neck from chin to core. Exhale through your mouth by blowing vigorously through slightly pursed lips to a slow count of 1-2, while deflating the lower abdomen and doing the following:

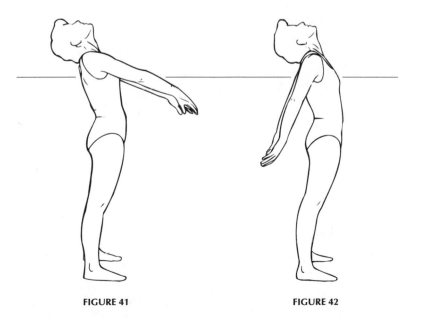

FIGURE 41   FIGURE 42

☐ On the first count, swing your arms forward, bringing your hands toward shoulder height (see Figure 41).

☐ On the second count, keeping your head back, swing your arms back as far as possible (see Figure 42).

4. Place the tip of your tongue against your top front teeth. Bend your head forward as far as possible to stretch the back of your neck. Inhale intensely through your nose to a slow count of 1-2, while inflating the lower abdomen and doing the following:

☐ On the first count, swing your arms forward toward shoulder level (see Figure 43).

☐ On the second count, keeping your head bent, swing your arms back as far as possible (see Figure 44).

5. Repeat steps 3 and 4 seven times.

6. Relax by rotating your shoulder joint and gently shaking your arms and legs.

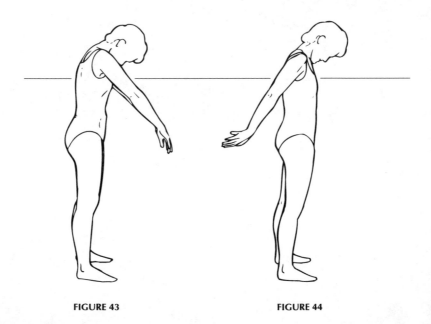

FIGURE 43   **FIGURE 44**

EXERCISE 3D

Leading the Breath to the Core

This long, detailed exercise is divided into two sections. Steps 1 through 7 aim to reveal more completely the location of the core and its cradle through a back-arching movement that induces the lower abdominal wall to stretch as it deflates during exhalation. This movement establishes a strong awareness of the core. After the lower abdomen is completely deflated, you will forcefully expand it, drawing a big gulp of air into the core and its surrounding area. Steps 8 through 10 take advantage of techniques learned in Lesson 1 by repeating deep breathing in a relaxed standing position. Read through the instructions several times so that you understand the steps and will be able to perform the exercise comfortably and easily.

1. Stand up straight with your feet 12 to 14 inches apart and your toes pointed slightly outward. Place your hands on the lower abdominal wall, palms inward, fingers almost touching (see Figure 45).

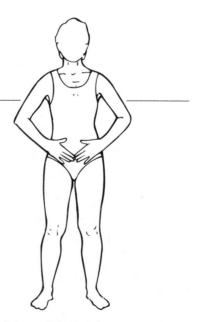

FIGURE 45

2. Place the tip of your tongue against your bottom front teeth. Exhale through your mouth by blowing gently through slightly pursed lips to a slow count of 1-2-3-4-5-6-7-8-9-10-11-12, while gradually deflating the lower abdomen and giving it a big squeeze inward as your breath is depleted

3. As you hold this deflated state, bend your head back with your chin upward (see Figure 46). Steps 3 through 5 should take only a few seconds, so no inhalation is necessary.

4. Bring your arms behind your back, joining your hands by interlocking the fingers. Rest your joined hands on your buttocks (see Figure 47.)

5. Arch back gradually while pushing your locked hands downward and tilting your chin high with your mouth closed. Be sure not to bend your knees (see Figure 48). As you continue to arch back in this manner, you will feel a very strong sensation in the lower abdomen.

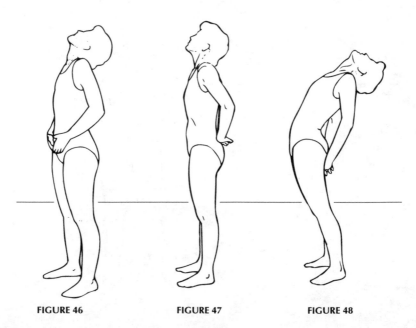

FIGURE 46　　　　　**FIGURE 47**　　　　　**FIGURE 48**

6. Give a strong squeeze inward with the lower abdominal muscles to expel the last traces of breath.

7. Immediately relax your tongue, resting it against your bottom front teeth, and inhale through your mouth, completely filling the core cradle (lower abdomen). Hold your breath for a few seconds, letting it sink deeply into the core and stabilize and anchor there.

As you continue with the second part of Exercise 3D, do not attempt, in step 8, to squeeze out air excessively. This excessive effort might shift the pivot point upward to the chest, completely undoing your accomplishment of locating the core in order to anchor the breath there.

8. Loosen all muscle tension. Slowly return to a normal standing position, letting your arms and hands dangle at your sides. Place the tip of your tongue against your bottom front teeth. Exhale slowly through your mouth, maintaining the sensation of being anchored. Stop the exhalation when your breath seems completely expelled from the lower abdomen.

9. Place the tip of your relaxed tongue against your slightly parted top and bottom front teeth. Inhale slowly and deeply through your nose, while inflating the lower abdomen. Continue to hold the tip of your tongue at the same position. Exhale slowly and deeply through your nose while deflating the lower abdomen.

10. Repeat step 9 three times.

11. Relax, and rest.

12. Repeat this exercise, steps 1 through 11, two or three times. Rest between each repetition.

Thoughts on Lesson 3

Having completed Lesson 3, you should now be able to apply the abdominal deep-breathing technique to improve your daily breathing. Use the tongue position described in step 9 of Exercise 3D in your everyday breathing. For instance, as you watch TV, walk, exercise, or just relax, inflate and deflate your lower abdomen. Remember, inflate for inhalation and deflate for exhalation. The more you practice this technique, the more habitual it will become.

Since deep breathing stimulates and strengthens the core, it is advisable to do it as frequently as you can. At this stage, you should be able to sense the location of the core without great effort. Think frequently of its location, and familiarize yourself with its presence.

LESSON 4

Varying and Extending the Breath

All of the exercises in this book are carefully planned to accomplish specific purposes. It is impossible to design special exercises or to plan special lessons to suit each individual's needs. You have now learned enough about *chi yi* to feel free to repeat those exercises that you find to be especially beneficial, even though they may not be included in a particular lesson. But be careful not to overexert yourself. Allow sufficient rest time between exercises. Always stop to rest if you become dizzy.

In Lesson 4 and later lessons, unless otherwise specified, the term *inhale* will always mean breathing in through the nose with the tip of the tongue against the top front teeth, and *exhale* will always mean blowing out gently through slightly pursed lips with the tip of the tongue placed lightly against the bottom front teeth.

Tongue positions for inhalation and exhalation may now be executed more casually, as long as the tongue remains flexible and unobtrusive and is not tense, retracted, or lumping. As you review Exercise 2C in this lesson, apply the following image.

IMAGERY DRILL

Kite

Imagine controlling your tongue the same way you would fly a kite. You control your kite from the end of the string that you hold in your hand. But to control it well, under conditions of varying wind direction and intensity, you must have great dexterity in your hand.

Likewise, the capability of your tongue relies a great deal on how well you can control it from the core. Imagine your tongue as the kite, and control it from your core, way down in the center of your lower abdomen. You will discover how well your tongue can perform and respond. Apply this image in this lesson as you review Exercise 2C.

RECOMMENDED REVIEW   EXERCISES 3A AND 3B AND EXERCISE 2C

Lesson 4 begins with a review of anchoring the breath in four different positions: lying flat, sitting on the floor, sitting in a chair, and standing up. This review session is fairly strenuous. Be easy on yourself, and take a sufficient break before going on to Exercise 4A. Repeat each of the review exercises as many times as necessary to feel you have mastered them thoroughly.

EXERCISE 4A

Flexing the Lower Abdominal and Lower Back Muscles

In this doubled-up position, the tendons and muscles of the feet and legs are thoroughly stretched. This stretched sensation is passed on up to the base of the torso (the lower abdomen). In bending over, you further extend this sensation up your back to your neck and even to the top of your head. Your entire body is in a state of attention. Centralize all your attention at the core. Focusing in this way will induce your breathing to come and go from the core.

Exhaling while bending over squeezes air out of the abdomen. When you inhale as you sit up, air is drawn easily into the abdomen.

1. Kneel on the floor with your knees together; keep your back straight and sit on your heels. Place your hands in your lap, palms down, fingers pointing forward, and thumbs inward. Keep your elbows by your sides. Lower and relax your shoulders. Hold your head up straight, being careful not to lower your chin (see Figure 49). (If you find it difficult to sit on your heels, place a pillow or cushion on your heels and sit on that.)

FIGURE 49   **FIGURE 50**

2. Exhale to a slow count of 1-2-3-4-5-6-7-8-9-10, while doing the following steps simultaneously (see Figure 50):

   ☐ Bend forward from the hips, and curve your back.

   ☐ Bring your forehead slowly to the floor, or as low as possible.

3. Inhale rapidly to a slow count of 1-2-3, while doing the following steps simultaneously:

   ☐ Straighten up, returning to your original kneeling position (see Figure 51).

   ☐ Expand your lower abdomen and sides. Do not lift your shoulders or raise your chest. Straighten your neck and lift your head slightly.

4. Repeat steps 2 and 3 five times.

5. Sit up, breathe normally, relax for a moment, and proceed to the following segment.

FIGURE 51

EXERCISE 4A CONTINUED

This segment promotes inflation of the lower back torso. Exhaling while deflating all sides of the lower torso in an upright sitting position prepares you for your next inhalation. As you bend over while inhaling, the air you take in will significantly fill up the lower back as the front abdomen is being depressed.

1. Kneel on the floor with your knees together; keep your back straight and sit on your heels. Place your hands in your lap, palms down, fingers pointing forward, and thumbs inward. Keep your elbows at your sides. Lower and relax your shoulders. Hold your head up straight, being careful not to lower your chin (see Figure 52).

2. Exhale to a slow count of 1-2-3-4-5-6-7-8-9-10-11-12, while deflating the lower abdomen.

3. Inhale to a slow count of 1-2-3, while doing the following steps simultaneously (see Figure 53):

   □ Bend forward from the hips, bringing your forehead to the floor, or as low as possible.

   □ Inflate the lower back and sides.

FIGURE 52   FIGURE 53

4. Exhale to a slow count of 1-2-3-4-5-6-7-8-9-10, while doing the following steps simultaneously:

☐ Straighten up, returning to your original kneeling position (see Figure 54).

☐ Deflate the lower abdomen, back, and sides.

5. Repeat steps 3 and 4 five times.

6. Inhale, and return to the original step 1 position.

7. Exhale and relax.

Note: To help you visualize the deep breathing that involves inflating and deflating of the lower front, the lower back, and the lower sides simultaneously, from now on these areas will be called the *lower circumference* when spoken of as a unit.

RECOMMENDED REVIEW   EXERCISES 3B AND 3C

In preparation for Exercises 4C and 4D, this review of Exercises 3B and 3C serves primarily as a reminder of how to relax your neck and shoulders without losing your awareness of the core, the focal point of the flow of breath.

FIGURE 54

EXERCISE 4B

Flexing the Muscles of the Lower Sides and Back

Like Exercise 3A, Exercise 4B helps develop conscious control of a well-anchored breathing technique in a lying position. This exercise also develops the sides of the lower torso.

Practicing *chi yi* while lying in a twisted position will develop your ability to breathe properly in other twisted positions, whether sitting, standing, or moving.

1. Lie flat on your back with your feet 20 to 22 inches apart and your toes pointed. Your head should face the ceiling. Stretch your arms straight out to your sides, palms up (see Figure 55).

2. Exhale completely while deflating the abdomen.

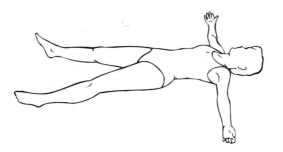

FIGURE 55

3. Inhale deeply while doing the following steps simultaneously (see Figure 56):

   □ Swing your right hand over in a semicircle and clap it to your left hand, turning your head toward the left.

   □ Inflate your abdomen, expanding the lower back and sides.

   □ Keep both heels stationary on the floor.

4. Exhale completely while doing the following steps simultaneously:

   □ Swing your right hand back over to the floor to its original position.

   □ Turn your head back to its original position (see Figure 55)

   □ Deflate your lower abdomen.

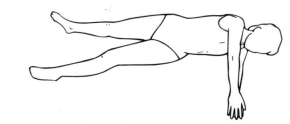

FIGURE 56

5. Inhale deeply while doing the following steps simultaneously (see Figure 57):

   ☐ Swing your left hand over in a semicircle and clap it to your right hand, turning your head toward the right.

   ☐ Inflate your abdomen, expanding the lower back and sides.

6. Exhale completely while doing the following steps simultaneously:

   ☐ Swing your left hand back over to the floor to its original position (see Figure 55).

   ☐ Turn your head back to its original position facing the ceiling.

   ☐ Deflate your lower abdomen.

7. Repeat steps 3 through 6 five times.

8. Lie stretched out on floor, and relax.

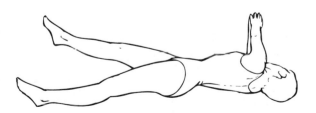

FIGURE 57

Developing Agility of the Abdominal and Lower Torso Muscles

After completing the neck-shoulder-upper torso relaxation exercises, you should now be ready to add movements that will relax the tongue as well.

Without tension in the neck, shoulders, and upper torso, tongue movement will automatically be controlled by the tongue's roots at the core.

Both the *toh* and *pah* are nonvocal, aspirated, exploding sounds.

1. Stand up straight with your feet 10 to 12 inches apart and your toes pointed slightly out.

2. Place your hands against the lower abdominal wall, palms inward, fingers almost touching, to monitor abdominal wall movements.

3. Place the tip of your tongue firmly against your top front teeth. Inhale deeply and fully. Make an explosive staccato *toh* sound, while snapping the lower abdominal wall inward (see Figure 58).

4. Take a quick, short breath through your nose, while rapidly expanding the lower circumference.

5. Immediately close your mouth, and follow with an exploding staccato *pah* sound while snapping the lower abdominal wall inward.

Note: Do not retract your tongue into the back of the mouth cavity when exploding the *toh* or *pah*. Drop your jaw to assist the rapid opening of the mouth for exploding sounds.

6. Repeat steps 3 through 5 twelve times.

7. Take a slow, deep breath, exhale and relax.

FIGURE 58

EXERCISE 4D

Expanding the Base of the Torso

Now that your lower torso's agility is well developed by the previous exercises, let your upper torso be consciously involved in the breathing process, taking care to maintain your attention and weight consistently in the lower torso. The top and bottom parts of the torso must be very carefully balanced to avoid a tendency toward top-heaviness.

Spreading your arms expands the torso top. Keeping your feet wide apart while bending and unbending the knees prevents loss of awareness of the core.

1. Stand up straight with your feet spread apart a few inches wider than shoulder width. Point your toes slightly outward.

2. Stretch your arms outward to the sides, level with your shoulders. Turn your palms down with your fingers together and extended straight out (see Figure 59).

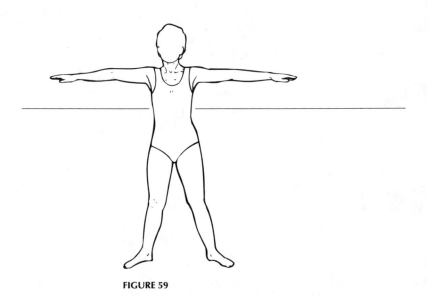

FIGURE 59

3. Inhale rapidly to a slow count of 1-2 and do the following steps simultaneously:

   ☐ Bend your knees outward over your toes (see Figure 60).

   ☐ Keep your elbows stationary and level with your shoulders, and swing your forearms in toward your collarbone. Join your fingertips; your fingers should meet a few inches below your chin.

   ☐ Keep your torso straight; do not allow your buttocks to stick out.

4. Exhale rapidly to a slow count of 1-2, deflating the abdomen and returning to your starting position, standing straight with arms outstretched and pointing out to opposite sides (see Figure 59).

5. Repeat steps 3 and 4 ten times.

6. Repeat step 3, and hold for 5 seconds.

7. Straighten your legs and let your arms dangle at your sides. Exhale slowly, deflate the abdomen, and relax.

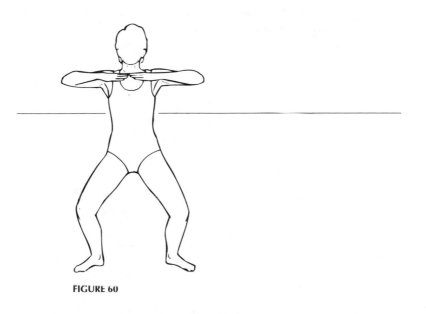

FIGURE 60

Thoughts on Lesson 4

The exercises in this lesson emphasize the lower sides of the torso (the lower waist) by inducing air to these areas with appropriate postures and movements. With your lower abdomen and lower back deflatable and inflatable, your sides should now also be as flexible. Your lower torso is now expandable in four dimensions, forming the lower circumference.

The lower circumference, together with your torso base, envelops the cradle of the core. External stimulation by the lower circumference activates your core to radiate inner energy throughout your entire being.

Throughout this book, we have often used vivid mental pictures to help you visualize how your body functions. If a certain mental image works for you, use it whenever you wish to overcome difficulties. If the following Coil of Rope Imagery Drill, or any other, helps you with your exercises, use it frequently until the effect wears off, and then substitute or invent another one.

IMAGERY DRILL

Coil of Rope

Imagine air entering and leaving your abdomen as a coil of rope with the bottom circle always remaining at the core.

LESSON 5

Using the Breath to Develop the Core

This lesson includes more review exercises than any previous lesson. It is important, at this advanced stage, to take the time to reexamine how each of these exercises induces the manner of breathing we seek. A thorough understanding of how certain movements and positions help induce specific breathing mechanisms will build confidence for improvisation in the future.

If you lack time or energy, it is better to cut down the number of repetitions in the review exercises than to skip any exercise entirely, since the order of the exercises—including the reviews—is designed to lead smoothly and effectively from one to the next.

RECOMMENDED REVIEW   EXERCISES 4A AND 4B

Review Exercises 4A and 4B, repeating each one as many times as necessary to accomplish their objectives effectively. You should now be able to perform these exercises more efficiently and meaningfully than you did when they first appeared in the previous lesson.

EXERCISE 5A

Further Expanding the Lower Circumference

The movements in this exercise are very simple. Their purpose is to practice control of the breath flow, extending exhalation time and shortening inhalation time. In speech and singing, we inhale rapidly and exhale slowly to enable the breath to be sustained through a phrase.

A slight dizziness may occur at step 7 if you stand upright too rapidly, or if you are unaccustomed to bending over. Relax, and the feeling will quickly pass.

As you stand and bend over as far as possible, the weight of the torso is borne at and suspended from the torso base. In this position, it is easy to breathe automatically to the core.

During this exercise, be sure to keep track of the pace of your breathing so that you can sustain your exhalation for an extended time.

1. Stand up straight with your feet 18 to 20 inches apart and your toes pointed slightly outward.

2. Place your hands at your waist with palms inward and thumbs pointed toward the back (see Figure 61).

FIGURE 61

3. Bend over gradually from the hips as far as possible (see Figure 62). Simultaneously, exhale by making the sound *"tse"* as in Exercise 2C to a slow count of 1-2-3-4-5-6-7-8-9-10-11-12, while gradually pulling the abdominal wall inward (deflating).

4. Inhale deeply and fully to a slow count of 1-2, while expanding the lower circumference.

5. Gradually stand back up and simultaneously exhale by again making the sound *"tse"* to the slow count of 1-2-3-4-5-6-7-8-9-10-11-12 while deflating your lower abdomen (see Figure 63).

6. Inhale fully, inflating lower abdomen.

7. Repeat steps 3, 4, 5, and 6 five times. Monitor inflation and deflation of your sides with your hands.

8. Exhale slowly, as you lower your hands to your sides.

9. Take a deep breath, and hold it at the core for a few seconds.

10. Relax and return to normal breathing.

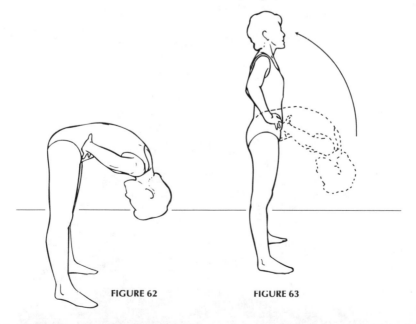

FIGURE 62   FIGURE 63

After practicing regulating your breath flow in Exercise 5A, you should be able to perform Exercise 2C with much more understanding and skill. This can be made more beneficial by lengthening the *tse* sound by as many counts as possible. It will be interesting for you to test your own endurance.

Make sure that as you use your tongue to produce the *tse* sound you do not tighten your neck and shoulder muscles or unconsciously allow your anchored base (core) to rise. Keep that base low.

EXERCISE 5B

Developing Core Sensation

This exercise focuses on a part of the anatomy that is seldom discussed in Western physical exercise programs. The rectal muscle is a sensitive part of the torso base. When this muscle is tightened at the same time as you swallow, you will feel a direct connection between the base of the core cradle and the opening of the throat. Combining this sensation with regulated exhalation creates an intense awareness of the core.

Pointing your toes downward and pushing your heels upward as indicated in step 5 of the following exercise will intensify the strength that emanates from the lower circumference.

Lowering your feet slowly to the floor as indicated in step 8 results in the greatest awareness of the core.

1. Lie flat on the floor. Place your hands by your sides, palms down, keeping your straightened legs together and pointing your toes (see Figure 64).

2. Inhale deeply and fully to a slow count of 1-2-3 while inflating the lower abdomen.

3. Hold your breath.

FIGURE 64

4. Keeping them together, lift both feet toward the ceiling. (If you have difficulty lifting your feet with your legs straight, bend your knees toward your chest and then straighten your legs upward, allowing your knees to be bent slightly.)

5. Point your toes downward while pushing your heels upward (see Figure 65).

6. Tighten the rectal muscle.

7. Place the tip of your tongue firmly against your front teeth, and swallow.

8. Maintaining the position described in steps 4 through 6, exhale to a slow count of 1-2-3-4-5-6-7-8-9-10, while lowering your legs slowly to their original position on the floor (see Figure 66).

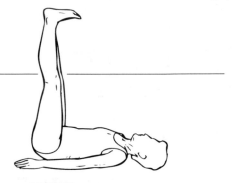

FIGURE 65

9. Inhale rapidly and deeply to a slow count of 1-2-3.

10. Remain lying down, and hold your breath for 3 seconds.

11. Exhale, and relax for a moment as you monitor the pulsing energy throbs in your core and even other areas of your body where *chi* is needed to help your building and healing process.

12. Repeat steps 2 through 11 two more times.

13. Breathe deeply several times, and relax.

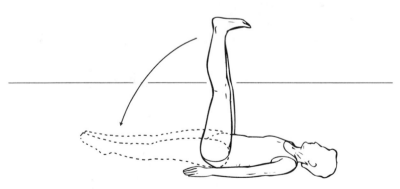

FIGURE 66

EXERCISE 5C

Expanding and Stabilizing the Breath at the Core

Like Exercise 4D, this exercise encourages the top, middle, and lower torso—including the entire length of the lungs—to be well-balanced and to function as a whole.

The arm movements help expand and relax the torso. Standing on tiptoe brings strength to the torso base.

1. Stand up straight with your feet 8 to 10 inches apart. Let your arms and hands dangle at your sides (see Figure 67).

2. Exhale completely to a slow count of 1-2-3-4-5-6-7-8-9-10, deflating the lower abdomen.

3. Inhale fully to a slow count of 1-2-3-4, inflating the lower circumference, while doing the following simultaneously (see Figure 68):

   ☐ Lift up your heels and stand on tiptoe.

   ☐ Raise your arms out to your sides at shoulder level.

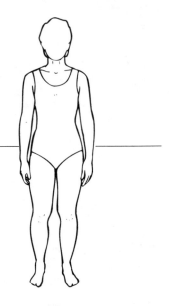

FIGURE 67

4. Exhale completely to a slow count of 1-2-3-4-5, deflating the lower abdomen, while doing the following simultaneously:

   ☐ Lower your heels to the floor, and stand flat on your feet.

   ☐ Lower your arms to your sides.

5. Inhale fully to a slow count of 1-2-3-4-5, inflating the lower circumference and doing the following simultaneously (see Figure 69):

   ☐ Lift up your heels and stand on tiptoe.

   ☐ Raise your arms forward and upward toward the ceiling.

6. Exhale completely to a slow count of 1-2-3-4-5-6-7, deflating the lower abdomen, and doing the following simultaneously:

   ☐ Lower your heels to the floor, and stand flat on your feet.

   ☐ Lower your arms to your sides.

7. Repeat steps 3 through 6 eight times.

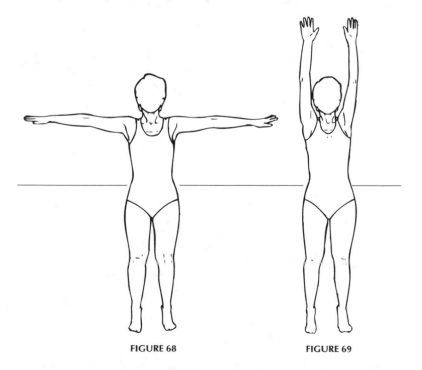

FIGURE 68   **FIGURE 69**

EXERCISE 5D

Intensifying Core Sensation

This exercise puts the rectal muscle into action once more.

Tightening your fists in conjunction with contracting the rectal muscle focuses a pivotal energy at the core, spreading upward to the diaphragm.

When tightening your fists, take care not to tighten your shoulders and neck; in that area tension will obstruct air flow into the bottom of the lungs.

1. Stand up straight with your feet 12 to 14 inches apart. Let your arms dangle.

2. Exhale to a slow count of 1-2-3-4-5-6-7-8, doing the following steps simultaneously:

   □ Slowly bend forward at the hips as far as possible, keeping your knees straight (see Figure 70).

   □ Deflate the lower abdomen.

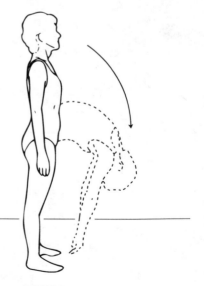

FIGURE 70

3. Holding the bent-over position, place your palms on your knees, fingers pointing inward. Bend your elbows and spread them outward (see Figure 71).

4. Inhale to a slow count of 1-2-3-4-5-6-7, doing the following steps simultaneously:

   □ Stand up slowly to an upright position.

   □ Raise your hands to head level, palms facing forward in front of your face, with your elbows still bent and spread.

5. Bring your palms to the sides of your head with your arms bent at right angles. Close your palms into tight fists (see Figure 72). Contract the rectal muscle, drawing it slightly upward.

FIGURE 72

FIGURE 71

6. Place the tip of your tongue against your top front teeth. Hold your head erect, tilting it back slightly. Swallow.

7. Immediately exhale as slowly as possible, doing the following steps simultaneously:

   ☐ Blow very slowly

   ☐ Rock your head left, right, left, and right to relax your head and shoulder muscles.

   ☐ Keep your fists tight, and gradually straighten your arms and lower your fists to your sides.

   ☐ Keep the rectal muscle contracted and drawn upward.

8. Continue exhaling slowly. You should be able to feel your core and all the muscles of your lower circumference tightening and exuding energy. Maintain muscle control until your breath is depleted.

9. Loosen your fists. Inhale and exhale deeply several times.

10. Repeat this exercise two more times, with a rest interval between repetitions.

11. Monitor the energy in your core and practice channeling it throughout your body.

Thoughts on the First Five Lessons

Having completed the first five lessons, you should have a clear inner vision of the location of the core, the primary objective of deep breathing. At this advanced stage of exercise, because of your increased awareness of disciplined breathing, you will no longer be given exact breath counts. Inhalation and exhalation can now be more relaxed and spontaneous. These less detailed directions will allow you greater flexibility and an opportunity to experiment sensibly and to adjust these exercises to fit your individual abilities.

You need no longer exaggerate abdominal inflation and deflation. The muscles of the lower circumference should by now be flexible, responsive, and sensitive. Flexing them even slightly should evoke an effective response. However, occasional conscientious repetition of the earlier exercises will prevent these muscles from becoming sloppy and unresponsive.

LESSON 6

Applying the Breath

In the twenty exercises of the first five lessons, we have covered just about all the important muscular maneuvers that can help induce abdominal deep breathing and lead to an awareness of core energy.

Lesson 6 includes many earlier exercises, reviewing them to reveal further benefits that might not have been obvious during previous executions.

The following imagery drill is designed to deepen your inhalations and extend your exhalations.

IMAGERY DRILL

Book Stacking

Form the mental image of inhaling as a process of stacking books. You start stacking at the bottom, adding books to build a pile. The taller the stack, the more weight the bottom book has to bear. For exhalation, you unload the books from the top, working your way to the bottom book, which remains until the very end. You can stack or unstack rapidly or slowly, so long as you do the job steadily.

From now on, the position of the tip of your tongue as you breathe is less critical, as long as the tip of the tongue touches the front teeth. This position ensures that the tongue is not pulled back to obstruct the flow of air at the back of the throat. A relaxed tongue is always important in deep breathing.

The imagery drill that follows tests your ability to apply the energy that your core can now generate.

IMAGERY DRILL

Facial Glow

Hold a mirror in front of you, and look into it. Take an easy, deep breath, and exhale. Look deeply into your own eyes as you take a long, deep breath and exhale. Put the mirror down, but keep your eyes straight ahead.

Think about smiling. Take another easy deep breath, and exhale. Sweep your glance upward, tilting your head back as you inhale deeply through your nose. Hold your breath, and let it surround your core for a moment.

Exhale slowly and steadily through your nose as you imagine a warm glow emanating from your core. At the same time, sweep your glance back down, and level your head. Break into a big smile, think a happy thought, and complete your exhalation. Inhale and exhale as you smile. Feel your eyes sparkle, grow warm, and shine. You are looking radiant!

Relaxed and content, proceed to Exercise 6A.

EXERCISE 6A

Spreading the Breath to the Base of the Torso

A cross-legged sitting position induces maximum awareness of the lower torso base as a result of the tension that is concentrated there. The tension is produced by assembling the torso weight and the weight of the four limbs at a single pivot platform that supports the entire body. Many people are unaccustomed to the cross-legged position; its awkwardness and discomfort make them more aware of that area.

When you are sitting in the cross-legged position, your shoulders may tense up. By resting your forearms on bent knees, you can thwart that tendency and keep the weight focused downward. In this position, whether you are inhaling or exhaling, imagine yourself as a pyramid that is stable and firmly anchored.

If you find it difficult or uncomfortable to sit cross-legged on the floor, you may sit on one or more firm cushions or on a low stool with your legs crossed in front. Place your hands palm down on your knees or in your lap with your fingers pointing inward.

1. Sit up straight in a cross-legged position. Bend your arms, resting your forearms on your knees. Join your hands by interlocking your fingers (see Figure 73).

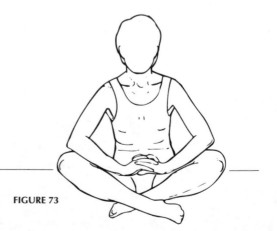

FIGURE 73

2. Place the tip of your tongue against your bottom front teeth. Exhale through your nose to a slow count of 1-2-3-4, while deflating the lower abdominal wall.

3. Place the tip of your tongue against your top front teeth. Inhale through your nose to a slow count of 1-2-3-4-5, while bending forward gradually as far as possible, directing your head toward the floor, and inflating your lower back torso. Let your forearms press on your knees to assist in lowering your knees toward the floor (see Figure 74). (If you are sitting in an elevated position on a cushion or stool, let your elbows and arms spread out and forward.)

4. Place the tip of your tongue against your bottom front teeth. Exhale through your mouth to a slow count of 1-2-3-4, while slowly returning to your original position and relaxing the forearm pressure on your knees. Do not deflate the lower abdominal wall; let the lower back wall react naturally to the sitting up motion.

5. Repeat steps 3 and 4 five times.

6. Remain sitting upright. Breathe freely and relax.

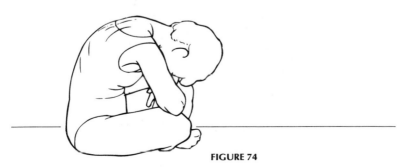

FIGURE 74

EXERCISE 6B

Strengthening the Abdominal Muscles

Raising your arms high and pointing your fingers upward helps you stretch the entire length of your torso as much as possible.

Spreading your feet far apart helps broaden and stabilize the torso base, but in doing so you risk swaying your back and curving out the lower spine. To minimize this risk, stretch your entire top body up as straight as possible. At the same time, pull your abdomen slightly inward even before exhalation begins .

1. Stand up straight with your feet apart a few inches wider than shoulder width. Point your toes slightly outward.

2. Raise your arms high, stretching your fingers toward the ceiling, palms forward (see Figure 75).

3. Exhale completely, doing the following steps simultaneously:

FIGURE 75

☐ Bend over and touch your toes (see Figure 76). If you can't touch your toes, bend as far as you can.

☐ Deflate the lower abdomen.

4. Inhale slowly, filling from the bottom up, doing the following steps simultaneously:

   ☐ Stand up slowly, stretching your arms and hands above your head (see Figure 77).

   ☐ Inflate the lower circumference.

5. Repeat steps 3 and 4 three times.

6. Remain standing with your hands reaching high.

7. Hold still for 3 seconds; then lower your hands to your sides.

8. Exhale completely, inhale deeply, and breathe freely as you continue onward with the following segment.

FIGURE 77

FIGURE 76

EXERCISE 6B CONTINUED

Strengthening the Lower Back Muscles

Notice that the emphasis in this segment shifts from the abdomen to the lower back torso by reversing the inhalation-exhalation procedure.

1. Stand up straight with your feet still apart a few inches wider than shoulder width. Point your toes slightly outward.

2. Raise your arms high above your head, stretching your fingers toward the ceiling, palms forward (see Figure 78). Exhale completely through your mouth.

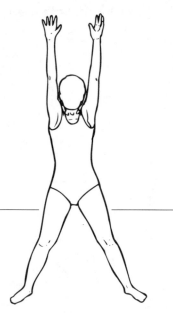

FIGURE 78

3. Inhale slowly from the bottom up, doing the following simultaneously:

   ☐ Bend over and touch your toes (see Figure 79). If you can't touch your toes, bend as far as you can.

   ☐ Inflate the lower circumference.

4. Exhale completely through your mouth, doing the following simultaneously:

   ☐ Stand up slowly, stretching your arms and hands toward the ceiling.

   ☐ Deflate the lower abdomen.

5. Repeat steps 3 and 4 three times.

6. Remain standing with your arms stretched high.

7. Hold your breath for a second.

8. Lower your hands, inhale deeply, exhale steadily, relax and breathe freely.

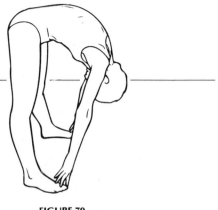

FIGURE 79

REVIEW EXERCISE 3A, EXERCISE 4A, AND EXERCISE 3D

Exercises 3A, 4A, and 3D demonstrate a progression of postures. Apply the following imagery drill during your review.

IMAGERY DRILL

Cream

Create a mental picture of an inhaled breath that is a rich, heavy liquid. On exhaling, leave behind the richness, and let the creaminess stick to the core, where it is converted into energy. You are learning to regulate and absorb that precious energy.

EXERCISE 6C

Strengthening the Diaphragm Muscle and the Core

The breathing action that accompanies this movement thoroughly exercises the diaphragm and stimulates the core.

Steps 3 and 4 may seem difficult. Simply alternate moving your fists up and down as you swing your hips. Bending your knees and tipping your toes helps maintain balance and accommodate easy swaying. In this movement the midtorso, where the diaphragm is located, is being squeezed and stretched on alternate sides to develop flexibility.

1. Stand up straight with your feet spread apart to the width of your shoulders. Raise your arms out to the sides at shoulder height; then bend your elbows upward at right angles. Keep your elbows level with your shoulders. Tighten your hands into fists, palms facing forward (see Figure 80). Exhale completely, deflating the lower abdomen.

2. Inhale slowly, deeply, and fully. Hold your breath. Tighten the rectal muscle, pulling slightly upward. Then swallow, maintaining core tension.

FIGURE 80

3. Keep your rectal muscle tight while blowing forcefully in two consecutive big puffs, deflating the lower abdomen. At the first puff, simultaneously:

   □ Pull your right fist downward, and push your left fist upward.

   □ Swing your right hip to the right.

   □ Bend your left knee slightly forward, raising your left foot on tiptoe (see Figure 81).

   At the second puff, simultaneously:

   □ Push your right fist upward, and pull your left fist downward.

   □ Swing your left hip to the left.

   □ Bend your right knee slightly forward, raising your right foot on tiptoe (see Figure 82).

4. Inhale through your nose forcefully in two consecutive sniffs, inflating the lower abdomen. At the first sniff, simultaneously:

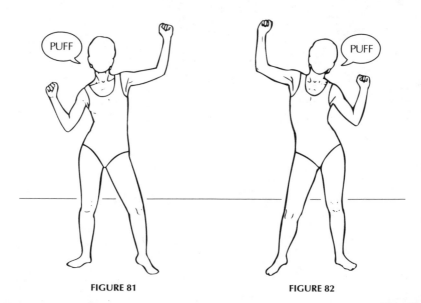

FIGURE 81   FIGURE 82

☐ Pull your right fist downward, and push your left fist upward.

☐ Swing your right hip to the right.

☐ Bend your left knee slightly forward, raising your left foot on tiptoe (see Figure 83).

At the second sniff, simultaneously:

☐ Push your right fist upward, and pull your left fist downward.

☐ Swing your left hip to the left.

☐ Bend your right knee slightly forward, raising your right foot on tiptoe (see Figure 84).

5. Repeat steps 3 and 4 ten times, maintaining a tightened rectal muscle. End with an inhalation; level your shoulders and elbows.

6. Exhale slowly, lowering your hands to your sides.

7. Inhale, exhale, relax, and breathe freely.

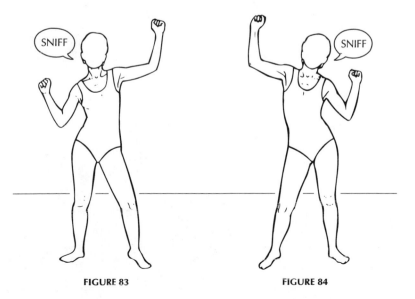

FIGURE 83   FIGURE 84

Exercise 6C was a rigorous exercise that placed great emphasis on the midtorso. Forgetting the lower torso and core can make it difficult for the breath to reach its necessary depth. A review of Exercises 5D and 5C will readjust any displacement that may have occurred. Exercise 5C will leave your body ready for Exercise 6D.

EXERCISE 6D

Jogging in Place with Chi Yi

All movement is affected by our manner of breathing. Jogging in place offers *one example* of the application of *chi yi*, showing how, in combination with various stages of physical exercise, you can experiment for improved results through the proper coordination of breathing and exercise.

1. Stand up straight with one foot flat on the floor and the other raised on tiptoe in a stationary jogging position. Keep your arms and hands in a position comfortable for running. Your hands should be loose and relaxed (see Figure 85).

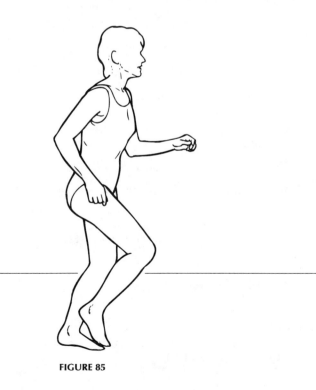

FIGURE 85

2. Throughout this exercise you will breathe in a natural way through the point where the back of the nose and the throat meet. Hold your teeth slightly apart, with your jaws relaxed. Place the tip of your tongue lightly behind your bottom front teeth.

3. Begin stationary jogging, slowly and steadily. Deflate the lower abdomen when exhaling, and inflate the lower circumference when inhaling. Alternately exhale and inhale in the following pattern:

   ☐ Exhale smoothly and steadily for 4 steps.

   ☐ Inhale smoothly and deeply for 4 steps.

   ☐ Exhale smoothly and steadily for 6 steps.

   ☐ Inhale smoothly and deeply for 6 steps.

   ☐ Exhale smoothly and steadily for 8 steps.

   ☐ Inhale smoothly and deeply for 8 steps.

   ☐ Exhale smoothly and steadily for 10 steps.

   ☐ Inhale smoothly and deeply for 10 steps.

   ☐ Exhale smoothly and steadily for 8 steps.

   ☐ Inhale smoothly and deeply for 8 steps.

   ☐ Exhale smoothly and steadily for 6 steps.

   ☐ Inhale smoothly and deeply for 6 steps.

   ☐ Exhale smoothly and steadily for 4 steps.

   ☐ Inhale smoothly and deeply for 4 steps.

   ☐ Exhale smoothly and steadily for 10 steps.

   ☐ Inhale smoothly and deeply for 10 steps.

4. As you continue stationary jogging, slowly and easily adapt to your normal breathing pattern while bringing your steps gradually to a standstill.

Thoughts on Lesson 6

The most important objective of this lesson is to develop a keener awareness of the core and to apply this awareness to *any* activity. By the time you have completed this lesson, the muscles involved in *chi yi* should respond readily to your commands. Feel free to improvise new routines, and to incorporate what you have learned into your daily activities.

Frequently review those exercises that are most effective for you. Do not overlook or underestimate the exercises in the beginning lessons; each one has its particular value.

Be patient and persistent in your practice and application of *chi yi*. Your painstaking effort at the beginning will gradually become spontaneous, and eventually you will find shallow breathing to be uncomfortable, ineffective, and unnatural. It is then that you will recognize that you have mastered the art of breathing.

You may have noticed that your natural breathing patterns sometimes have suspended (rest) intervals between exhalations and inhalations. The length of these suspended intervals depends mainly on the physical and sometimes on the mental and emotional demands at the time. A natural instinct usually takes care of such adjustments. For instance, in running the intervals will be very short. In walking, you may experience an interval to a count of 1 or 2, depending on the amount of energy exerted and the amount of air inhaled and exhaled. In resting, you may experience 3 counts inhale, 3 counts exhale, 3 counts suspended interval. When you are asleep, the suspended period will be extended. Understanding this fact will facilitate the adaptation of *chi yi* into whatever you do.

PART THREE

Applications of Chi Yi

Using the Core Energy

Once you have completed the six lessons outlined in Part 2 of this book, you will have established a strong, sound foundation in *chi yi*. As with all worthwhile skills, the techniques involved must be consistently practiced to maintain the art of breathing. Successful results depend on continued effort and mastery of all the lessons.

Now that your core awareness is well established, you are equipped to function more effectively in every area of your life. The applications that follow will show you how *chi yi* techniques may be applied to the endeavors of daily life, and how they enhance the health and well-being of those who practice them. Once you have worked with these applications, you will be able to adapt them to create your own program of *chi yi* practice.

Disciplined inner energy helps you to realize your full human potential. Uncontrolled inner energy creates tension and stress. It is impossible simply to discard unwanted tension and stress. You must *relocate* them. The practice of *chi yi* enables you to direct unwanted tension and stress to the core, from which it can be circulated throughout the body as beneficial energy.

Now that you have mastered the basic techniques of *chi yi* set forth in the progressive exercises of Part 2, the Steam Funnel Imagery Drill will further assist you in the circulation of inner energy. Keep this image in mind as you practice the applications in Part 3.

In this imagery drill, imagining your inhaled breath as water facilitates the feeling of the breath's flowing downward and hitting bottom. Imagining your exhaled breath as warm water and steam being pumped upward allows you to sense how the breath lingers during the exhalation. As you practice this exercise, you are likely to sense the warm inner energy flowing to your face and head area. Imagining the inner energy as a warm current provides a vivid sensation that can be easily traced and monitored.

Steam Funnel

Think of the back of your nose, at the point where it meets the throat, as the top of a funnel emptying into a long tube that leads all the way down to a focal area where a rotating propeller sits ready to spin (see Figure 86). As you begin an inhalation, imagine the air you breathe as water pouring into the funnel and draining down to start the rotor spinning. Let the rotor gain momentum for a few seconds, heating up and setting off an energy that radiates and sparkles and, at the same time, gives off enough power to propel an exhalation in the form of warm water and steam.

It is this return column of energized air that triggers and manipulates the voice. This energized exhalation also gives your face an attractive glow.

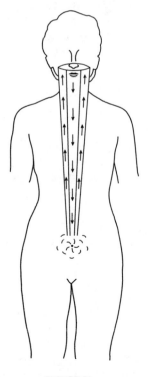

FIGURE 86

During exhalations, you gain the benefit of your inhalations, allowing you to target your inner energy to the body areas that need it most. You can most effectively direct your inner energy with your mind and imagination during the exhalation. You need not have a plan for every exhalation; most of the time it is natural to let your inner energy circulate freely so that your entire being can benefit from it.

Flourishing inner energy naturally attends to the most pressing needs of the various parts of your body. For instance, if you are extremely tired and lie down to rest, you may feel your inner energy throbbing at the parts of your body that are most strained, such as the base of your neck, your head, your legs, and so on. Encourage such sensations with *chi yi* breathing; they will help you to recuperate.

The surges of inner energy may be perceived as throbs, as patches of inner warmth, or as rays or flashes of inner light. These throbs are slower than the pulses of the heart, occurring about one per second or even more slowly. If these sensations come to you in the form of warm patches or light flashes and so have a less vivid rhythm, monitor them by mentally counting at the speed of roughly one count per second.

Whenever and wherever throbbing sensations occur—not painful ones—don't discourage them. They are a sign that your inner energy is surging to where it's needed in your body. For instance, if you have strained muscles at the base of your neck and in your shoulders, lie down and do *chi yi* breathing. Soon you will become aware of a throbbing sensation in that strained area, gradually bringing on relief and comfort.

After you have talked and smiled continuously for a long time, relax and focus your mind on your tired lips, jaws, gums, and on the back of your nose, and you will sense these muscles, bones, and tissues pulsating intensely. They are being helped by your inner energy to relax and recuperate.

When your eyes are tired or strained, close them and bring your attention to that area. Your eyes will be soothed with pulsating inner energy that will relax the eyes themselves and the surrounding muscles.

Painful throbbing is a signal from the body of some injury, tension, or stress. You will learn to blend these throbs with your inner energy surges to dispel pain and tension.

To encourage your awareness of the throbbing sensation created by the concentration of inner energy, practice the following imagery drill.

Sink and Drain

Inhale as if you are filling up a sink from the bottom upward. Exhale as if you are draining a sink through the bottom. Repeat these two steps a few times. Then suspend your breathing for a few seconds, and concentrate on developing a slow throb in your core. Resume breathing as you continue to monitor your throbs. Apply this throbbing sensation to various areas of the body by mentally moving the throbs from the core to other parts of your body.

Suggestions for Practicing the Applications

When you are practicing the applications, remember always to invigorate and back up your inner energy with deep inhalations and lingering exhalations. *Chi yi* breaths may vary in intensity and frequency. As you monitor your throbs, light flashes, or warm patches, your breaths may at times become so faint and infrequent that they seem hardly to be there.

These faint inhalations will be interspersed with some long, intense inhalations whenever your body feels the need. Let your natural instincts be your guide. If the throbs or sensations of light or warmth should hesitate or fade away, regenerate them with a few intense, regulated exhalations and inhalations, almost like deep sighs. Use the Sink and Drain Imagery Drill to encourage these sensations. Whether your breaths are faint or intense, frequent or sparse, the most important point to remember is to inhale to the core and to let your exhalations linger.

You can bring on the sensations of inner energy surges with *chi yi* breathing and exaggerated flexing of the lower abdominal muscles, which stimulates the core. Deep breathing can also be induced with vivid mental pictures, as in the imagery drill below.

IMAGERY DRILL

Drinking Straw

Imagine an oversized drinking straw with one end at the nose-- throat junction and the other end leading to the center of the core. Both ends are kept open at all times to allow the air to flow freely. As you inhale, imagine air being sucked in through the lower opening, inflating the lower abdomen. Stop, and reverse your mental gears in preparation for exhalation. Now imagine the straw with air flowing out through both ends (without collapsing the straw at any point). Exhale completely. Then proceed again with another inhalation .

The following core awareness imagery drill also cultivates and helps you channel the core's energy. It will be put to use in several of the applications that follow.

IMAGERY DRILL

Red Light Bulb

Do your *chi yi* breathing as you imagine, as vividly as you can, an electric socket at the location of your core. Screw a red light bulb into this socket, and watch it light up. Imagine that the light glows evenly as you exhale and inhale deeply and smoothly. At the pauses between exhalations and inhalations, or when you hold your breath, the light does not flicker or go out, but sustains an even glow.

As soon as *chi yi is* thoroughly integrated into your life, as you work or play or engage in physical activities throughout the day, you may apply an exercise or drill to help you relax or to act more effectively. Throughout the day and night, you will find yourself breathing more deeply, with greater ease. You are enjoying *chi yi*—the art of breathing.

APPLICATION 1

Promoting Relaxation

Whenever you are under pressure, or in a rush, or feeling tense, let *chi yi* help you take stock of the situation. Loosen and lower your shoulders. Breathe to your core, and let your breath linger and filter downward. Do this several times, until you feel your taut nerves and muscles loosen up. You will find that you are better able to control your feelings, and to be more patient, tolerant, and pleasant than before.

Anxiety can be greatly eased or even eliminated by bringing your inner energy throbs to the spot at the center of your chest just below the point where your front ribs meet. Concentrate your inner energy surges there, and let them warm that spot and loosen the knots there. Soon your anxiety will begin to evaporate.

1. Take a few deep breaths to firmly establish an inner vision of the core's location.

2. Analyze and trace your points of tension.

3. Continue breathing deeply and steadily as you direct imaginary lumps of tension, one at a time, to the core and calmly drop them into the core's cradle to dissolve.

4. Tension often gathers at the back of the neck and shoulders, contributing to aches and pains in the arms and from the head down through the spine. To relieve that neck-shoulder tension, check the following vital points, and follow the prescribed remedies.

   □ Tongue. If your tongue is persistently pulled back, away from the front teeth, tension will be created in the jaw and neck. Remedy this condition by pushing the tongue forward gently, filling up the space behind the lower front teeth. Then let the tongue go limp, and breathe.

   □ Shoulders. When your shoulders are heaved (raised), you are fighting against gravity. Seesaw and rotate your shoulders a few times; then smooth your shoulders backward and downward, and breathe comfortably.

APPLICATION 2

Waking Up Alert: The Good Morning Regimen

For many people, just waking up and getting out of bed in the morning requires quite an effort and, in fact, may be very stressful. Many rely on a cup of black coffee or an extra half hour in bed to become their usual social selves. They hope to become alert, bright-eyed, and radiant as the day goes by.

This *chi yi* regimen prepares you for getting out of bed with all your faculties fully functioning. The regimen requires you to stay in bed for 10 minutes or so after you awaken. If you wake up by the alarm clock, set it 10 minutes earlier. You will get out of bed much less blurry-eyed and cranky than you would have after those extra 10 minutes of sleep. This *chi yi* application requires willpower on your part, but you will find the reward more than worth the effort.

At first glance, the regimen may look long and complicated. After you review it a few times, you will find it systematic and easy to remember. Memorize the steps or at least understand and organize them in your mind before you actually do the regimen.

The number of throbs indicated in this application is to be considered a guideline. Use your discretion in this matter according to your physical condition and the time you have allotted for performing the regimen. You can mentally direct inner energy sensations and channel them to whatever location you desire. For instance, if you have a stuffy nose, a sore throat, or an uncomfortable stomach, you will want to let the throbs linger in the sensitive area.

When you wake up in the morning, remain lying in bed with your eyes closed. If you need to make a trip to the bathroom, return immediately to bed. If your room is cool, keep the covers over you so that you are comfortable and warm. You may bend your knees if that position is more comfortable than lying flat. At first you may find lying on your back easier than any other position, but as you become more experienced, you may find it just as easy to perform the regimen lying on either side, as long as you are relaxed and comfortable.

Remember always to invigorate and back up your inner energy with deep inhalations and lingering exhalations.

1. Lie comfortably in bed with your eyes closed.

2. Do the Eyedropper Imagery Drill from Part 1 to refresh the deep breathing sensation.

3. Relax your hands and elbows. Rest your hands one over the other on your lower abdomen. Let your elbows rest on the bed beside your body.

4. Flex your lower abdominal muscles and vigorously deflate the abdomen as you exhale by blowing rapidly through slightly pursed lips. Relax your abdominal muscle; it will pop outward, effecting a rapid, deep inhalation of air. Do this in/out process of flexing the abdominal wall to the count of 1-2. Repeat the process 10 times in succession, ending with a long, slow, deep inhalation followed by a long, slow, thorough exhalation.

5. Relax. Monitor your body for throbs or pulsations. You may sense them at many areas of your body, especially around your eye sockets, between your cheeks and gums, at the back of your nose, and in your neck, your inner shoulders, and your lower abdomen. If you are aware of no such sensations, repeat step 4. If you still have no reaction, do the Simplified Vowel Exercise that appears on page 155. Then proceed to step 6.

6. Concentrate on throbs in one area at a time, starting with the lower abdomen. Mentally direct the throbs to your tailbone. Inch them slowly up the spine to the top of your head (the crown).

7. Mentally direct the throbs toward the eye sockets. Monitor 20 throbs there.

8. Direct 10 to 14 throbs to the center of the bridge of the nose. If you have a stuffy nose, let the throbs dwell longer at that area, and the stuffiness may disappear.

9. Direct 10 to 14 throbs to the tip of your nose.

10. Direct 10 to 14 throbs to your upper gum.

11. Let 10 to 14 throbs spread to your cheeks. You may feel a flush spreading through the center of your face. Direct 10 throbs to that area.

12. Direct 10 to 14 throbs each to your lower gum, tongue, and chin.

13. Direct 10 to 14 throbs to your throat. If you have a sore throat, allow the throbs to dwell at the throat area to soothe away the pain. If a ticklish feeling in the throat is bringing on a cough, hold off the cough as long as you can. Allow the throbs to dwell at that location until the tickling sensation subsides.

14. Direct 10 to 14 throbs to the base of the neck and across the inner shoulders. If you are suffering from a stiff neck or strained shoulders, let the throbs dwell in the neck-shoulder area to relieve tension.

15. Direct throbs in little steps, one throb per step, down the center front of your body. Let the throbs dwell at whatever spot feels tight, uncomfortable, or uneasy. Throbbing in the abdominal area may at times start your stomach rumbling; it may even cause you to pass gas. This response is a good sign; it shows that your stomach is waking up, too! Aim your throbs toward the lower abdomen.

16. Rub your warm hands over your abdomen and the front of your rib cage, gently massaging these areas. Enjoy this stimulation for a few seconds, or longer if you wish.

17. Sit up. Put your feet on the floor.

18. Dangle your head and roll it to the right in big circles slowly 4 times, synchronizing the motion with the breath— inhale-exhale-inhale-exhale. Repeat the process, rolling your head to the left.

19. Bring your right palm to the left side of the base of your neck. Pat gently and firmly, starting at the base of the neck, moving along the left shoulder and down the arm toward

the hand and fingers. Pat more at the spots where you feel tension. Repeat this patting motion 2 times.

Note: During the process of directing the inner energy surges up and down your head and torso in steps 1 through 16, your limbs may have become tense. The patting will relieve any tension. And more importantly, the stimulation of the patting will lead the flow of inner energy you have activated during steps 1 through 16 to the limbs as well.

20. Bring your left palm to the right side of the base of your neck. Pat gently and firmly, starting at the base of the neck, moving along the right shoulder and down the arm toward the hand and fingers. Again, pat more at any tense spots. Repeat this patting motion 2 times.

21. Again bring your right palm to the left side of the base of your neck. Pat along the shoulder to the top of the left arm. At this point, turn your left palm outward, bringing the inside of your left arm outward also. Continue patting downward along the inside of the left arm to the palm, ending at the fingertips. Repeat this patting motion 2 times.

22. Again bring your left palm to the right side of the base of your neck. Pat along the shoulder to the top of the right arm. At this point, turn your right palm outward, bringing the inside of your right arm outward also. Continue patting downward along the inside of the right arm to the palm, ending at the fingertips. Repeat this patting motion 2 times.

23. Stand up. Dangle your hands in front of you and shake them vigorously 20 times.

24. Stand up straight with your feet spread comfortably, 16 to 18 inches apart. Bring your right hand to your left underarm with the palm inward, fingers pointing backward. Gently and firmly pat downward on the left side of your body to the left hip; then proceed toward the center of your lower abdomen. Repeat this patting motion 2 times.

25. In the same standing position, bring your left hand to your right underarm with the palm inward, fingers pointing backward. Gently and firmly pat downward on the right side of your body toward the right hip, and proceed to pat toward the lower center of the abdomen. Repeat this patting motion 2 times.

26. Stand upright with your feet slightly parted, 8 to 10 inches apart. Bring your hands to the sides of your hips, palms inward, fingers pointing toward the center of your back. Gently and firmly pat slowly toward the center lower back, and proceed downward along the backs of your legs to your heels. Bend down gradually as you pat, then straighten up. Repeat this patting motion 2 times.

27. Bend forward with your feet parted at slightly wider than shoulder's width. Bring your hands to your crotch (the very top of the inside of your legs) with the palm inward, fingers pointing backward. Gently and firmly pat downward along the inside of your legs toward the inside ankles, bending down gradually as you pat. Stand up. Repeat this patting motion 2 times.

28. Walk in place or around the room 30 to 40 steps, lifting your feet high. Now you are all set for a good day, with bright eyes and rosy cheeks, full of energy.

Whenever you have the luxury of relaxing in bed for a few extra minutes, take the opportunity to improve your weak areas. For example, if you are susceptible to lower back pain, lie on your side with your knees drawn up in the fetal position. Focus your mind on your lower back. Take a few *chi yi* breaths, then direct your throbs (or patches of warmth, or flashes of light) to your lower back. Let these sensations dwell at the painful area for as long as you like. You may focus your mind on and send your inner energy to soothe and repair any spot in your body—a joint in your finger, a strained calf muscle, or your teeth and gums.

To start the day with a rosy glow, bring the throbs to your face in order to stimulate your skin and facial muscles.

APPLICATION 3

Motivating Movement from the Core

This application of *chi yi* shows you how to make connections between your movements and your core. Breathing affects your core, which in turn affects your movements. If you are lucky, your movements may be instinctively motivated from the core, whether or not you realize how that came about. However, the more fully you understand and exercise your ability to move from the core, the more you can control your movements and improve them at will.

After you have practiced this application, you will find that you are more aware of every movement you make, and you will move with more control. Your penmanship may even improve! At first, practice this application for short periods (5 to 10 minutes). This technique of control will gradually blend into your everyday movements, naturally and easily. Your movements will become more graceful, more steady, and more confident.

1. Stand with your feet 10 to 12 inches apart, toes pointed slightly outward. Hold your hands behind your back, and let them dangle loosely.

2. Inhale deeply, and exhale thoroughly. Inhale again easily, and continue breathing without further attention to your breathing process.

3. Tighten your lower abdominal muscle, and lift the center of the torso floor.

4. Do the Red Light Bulb Imagery Drill. Imagine as vividly as you can an electric socket at the location of your core. Screw a little red light bulb into this socket and watch it light up. Imagine the glowing bulb.

5. Raise on tiptoe and lower yourself several times. As you do this, imagine that the bulb glows with each lift. The more strength your movement requires, the brighter the bulb glows.

6. Place your feet more widely apart. Shift your weight from one foot to the other a few times. As you do this, imagine that the bulb glows more intensely as the movement demands greater energy.

7. Walk around the room. Imagine that the bulb brightens and dims as you pick up and lower your feet and shift your weight.

8. Raise one arm to your head. Notice the reactions of the bulb. Draw big round circles in the air with your hand. Lower your hand gracefully to your side. This movement also takes energy to control. Imagine how the bulb brightens and dims as any part of you moves. Raise your other arm, and put it through various motions. Pick up objects from the table, and put them back down. Mentally watch the reactions of the bulb.

9. Turn your head to one side. Lift it. Turn it to the other side. Keep an image of the bulb in your mind as you move.

10. Make any movement with any part of your body. Lift and wiggle a finger. Roll your eyes. Write with a pencil. Maintain the imagery of the bulb glowing in its various intensities.

APPLICATION 4

Developing Athletic Prowess

The previous application, which develops motivated movements, will adapt easily and beneficially to all your athletic activities. Athletic movements require much more exact execution, strength, and coordination than do the movements of everyday actions. At first you may feel that the application interferes with your spontaneity and natural reflexes; and it may, until you make the technique part of your subconscious mind. If practiced faithfully, however, this technique will soon become spontaneous, and will greatly enhance your athletic movements.

All sports require footwork of some sort. Your steps determine the direction, position, and maneuverability of your entire body. Experiments scrutinizing runners' patterns of running and breathing at various stages of a run, under various conditions, and at different speeds, have concluded that synchronization takes place between pace and breath. The speed of a runner depends on both the rate and the length of his or her stride. Experiments have shown that even when runners aim for a longer stride, their phase-locked pattern of breathing and footsteps need not change. Scientists are continuing to study phase-locked breathing and running patterns.

A 1983 article by Dennis M. Bramble and David R. Carrier (*Science*, Vol. 219, 21 January 1983, p. 251) recorded that four-legged animals normally synchronize their footfalls and their breathing cycles for trots and gallops at a constant 1:1 ratio (one stride per breath). Human runners employ several phaselocked patterns (4:1, 3:1, 2:1, 1:1, 5:2, 3:2), although the 2:1 pattern seems to be the most commonly used. In whatever pattern, the synchronization of breathing and physical movements appears to be necessary during sustained running.

If a phase-locked pattern of movement and breathing is necessary for sustained running, it must also be important for not-so-sustained running, and it may well be helpful in walking in regulated steps. In fact, a phase-locked pattern between breathing and any movement of the body can effect better performance. These patterns, however, vary under different conditions and with different people. No formula has been established for getting the best results. You, or you and your coach, will work out what is best for you.

Where does the runner get the extra energy required for longer strides? I believe that the principles of *chi yi* offer an answer to how the runner gets extra energy: Deeper breathing stimulates the core to produce more inner energy.

Sports vary greatly in their degree of rhythmic involvement. In general, noncompetitive sports—jogging, bicycling, aerobic exercises, rope skipping, skating, and so on—are more highly regulated by rhythm. Competitive sports that engage opponents and require teamwork—tennis, football, baseball, and so on—are usually freer from set rhythms. The more rhythmic the sport, the more your performance can benefit from phase-locked patterns of breathing and movement.

This application will show you how to generate and direct inner energy when participating in athletic activities.

1. Strike the stance that you would normally take as you begin practicing your sport.

2. If an instrument such as a racket is involved, hold it as you normally would at the starting point.

3. Take a *chi yi* breath (exhalation and inhalation).

4. Inhale, and hold your breath without straining. Touch your top and bottom teeth together, but don't bite hard. Place the tip of your tongue against your front teeth.

5. Produce a sustained *tse* sound. To make sure that this sound does not bring on tension of the neck or shoulder muscles, roll your head clockwise and counter-clockwise several times as you proceed with your continuous *tse* sound.

6. As you continue making the *tse* sound, you will feel your core tightening and generating energy. Sustaining the sound, think of the Red Light Bulb Imagery Drill with the bulb plugged into the socket. Imagine the light of the red bulb glowing steadily—as steady as your *tse*—until the end of this exhalation.

7. Inhale.

8. Exhale in the form of disconnected short *tse* syllables. As you exhale, do the following simultaneously:

   ☐ Do the movements of your sport—swing your racket, take a step, jump, swing, or the like—in a slightly slow motion.

   ☐ Accompany each movement with a *tse* sound and a profuse glow of the imaginary red bulb. (You can do this step when you are actually playing the game just for practice.)

9. Continue to inhale and exhale freely, at the rate and intensity at which you feel comfortable. As you exhale, the disconnected *tse* sounds should accompany your actions; let the core bulb glow to accompany your *tse* sounds.

10. Continue with steps 7, 8, and 9 as long as you wish and as long as you feel comfortable doing them.

APPLICATION 5

Sustaining Personal Presence

Most virtuoso performers are able to attract the attention of their audience, but the greatest virtuosos are those who can maintain a continuous magnetism so that members of the audience can't take their eyes or ears from them even when they pause. This ability to deliver a skill laced with continuous magnetism adds a charismatic quality to every note, phrase, line, and movement they send forth—a string of perfected pearls strung together not with string but with magnetic inner energy.

Applications 3 and 4 teach you to direct your inner energy to your physical expression and movements. This application shows you how to develop an inner energy capable of sustaining and molding itself so that it corresponds with the demands of artistic performance and stage presence. You may apply this energy to your performance in any situation, in the conference room or on the stage.

First, do the Red Light Bulb Imagery Drill. We will work with the image of the red electric bulb plugged in at your lower abdomen, at the location of your core. Not only must you be able mentally to turn it on and off, but when you are performing, you must know how to keep it on all the time. You don't want it at full power continuously; you want to be able to manipulate its glow as though it had a dimmer switch.

Basically, you must learn to overcome the break between exhalation and inhalation. Your imaginary bulb has a natural tendency to go off at that moment of transition, so that you must mentally make the light come back on after the interruption. This takes additional effort, and you may momentarily lose your audience.

This application helps you overcome the interference of this sporadic "darkness" in the breathing cycle. The steps sound simple, but the application is difficult; it can be mentally exhausting. Be careful not to overpractice, especially at first; 10 or 20 seconds may be enough for beginners. Eventually, however, the application will become a spontaneous part of your skill in appearing before people. Your diligence will be greatly rewarded.

1. Do the Red Light Bulb Imagery Drill.

2. Exhale, as you imagine the light burning brightly.

3. As you approach the end of your exhalation, mentally turn the light bulb to tighten its contact with the socket, and make sure that the light does not flicker, dim, or go off.

4. Inhale without the slightest flickering of the light. Continue inhaling, and keep the light shining.

5. As you approach the end of your inhalation, again mentally turn the light bulb slightly to reassert its contact with the socket. Make sure that the light does not flicker or dim.

6 Repeat steps 2 through 5 as many times as you can manage without overexerting mentally.

APPLICATION 6

Working through Pain

The painful throbs you experience when you are in pain are SOS signals for immediate attention. Do not ignore those throbbing pains. They are calling for the mind to direct inner energy to that area. When your mind focuses on an area of your body, inner energy can be directed to that place to perform its function of soothing, healing, and strengthening. The length of time it takes the pain to ebb away depends on the degree of affliction.

1. Take several deep, full inhalations and lingering, thorough exhalations.

2. Focus your mind on any throbbing pains. Monitor them by mentally counting as you continue with your *chi yi* breathing. Count in a simple sequence such as 1 through 4, or 1 through 10. Repeat the sequence to avoid high numbers with many syllables, which tend to interfere with a free-flowing rhythm.

3. Continue to count. Before long, you will find the pain subsiding and the throbs becoming regular and painless throbs of inner energy.

APPLICATION 7

Relieving Discomfort in the Fingers, Hands, and Arms

You can use *chi yi* to relieve muscle aches in the limbs. For example, if your elbow aches, bring on the inner energy throbbing sensation. Stimulate a few throbs of pain at the elbow by bending or pressing it. Synchronize the energy throbs with the painful throbs in your elbow, while letting your entire arm relax and go limp. Maintain your *chi yi* breathing. The throbs of pain will very quickly become plain throbs. Monitor the throbs at the elbow for at least 50 to 100 counts At the end of this count you will find your pain much relieved, if not completely gone. Your first few tries may not bring on very conspicuous positive results. Give this approach several chances, taking a little rest time between attempts. Repeat this therapy whenever necessary.

This application can be done while you are lying down, sitting, or standing and in any surroundings—in front of a TV set or in a concert hall—as long as your hands are free.

During this application, your inner energy will stimulate the painful areas and cut through any interference that may stagnate the flow of the inner energy current. Let us say, for example, that the joints in your left index finger are painful, due to strain or arthritis.

1. Warm your right hand in any convenient way. Put it in your pocket, or hold it under your coat or your sweater, or even in your armpit.

2. Wrap your warm right hand over your left index finger, gripping it firmly but without squeezing.

3. In seconds you will feel your left index finger throbbing together with your right hand. You are feeling the pulses of your heartbeat. These heart beats, at about 70 to 80 per minute, are faster than the throbs created by your inner energy, at about 45 to 55 per minute.

4. Monitor the heart-related throbs for about 30 seconds.

5. Loosen the grip of your right hand to an easy hold. Continue focusing your mind on your aching index finger.

6. The heart-related throbs will grow faint and, as they seem to be ebbing away, slower-paced throbs will emerge. Your inner energy surges are now taking over.

7. During steps 1 through 6 you have been breathing naturally in a *chi yi* manner and need not have given your breathing any thought. As you monitor the slower throbs, your breathing will adjust itself in rate, intensity, and quantity. At times your breathing may seem to have subsided to almost nothing; at other times you may feel the urge to take very deep, long inhalations. Let your instincts command your course. At this stage, you are equipped with adequate *chi yi* techniques to respond to any demand of breathing. If your inner energy throbs start to fade too soon, intentionally initiate several deep, long inhalations and lingering exhalations, which should strengthen the throbs again.

8. When you feel you can no longer concentrate or that the throbs have done their work, stop and relax.

9. During steps 6, 7, and 8, the pain in your finger should gradually have been eased and perhaps even eliminated. Although your finger may not hurt anymore, it may still feel stiff. Flex your left hand a few times, and massage it with your right.

10. Continue practicing this application frequently, with the intention of improving the condition of the ailing joints and preventing the recurrence of pain.

This approach to easing pain may also be practiced on your knees and upper thighs when you are in a sitting position and your hands can comfortably reach these areas.

APPLICATION 8

Conditioning the Legs and Arms

Our limbs are indispensable for a physically active life. For athletes, dancers, laborers, and many others, limbs are tools of the trade. Even when our limbs are healthy, it's still a good idea to give them some attention. We should develop the ability to lead our inner energy through our legs and arms, first to keep them healthy, and second to become familiar with the technique of directing inner energy through these areas. Then when our limbs need conditioning, soothing, or healing, we will be more adept and efficient at that task.

You can do this application while you watch TV or ride a bus, train, or plane, you can even do it during a dull lecture or conference, if no one is watching—you may look a little absent-minded. You can practice it while lying in bed, although if you are sitting up, it is easier for you to keep your eyes on the areas on which your mind's eye will also concentrate.

When you are thoroughly familiar with this application, you will not need the assistance of your eyesight to guide the movement of inner energy. You can direct and control the flow of inner energy with your mind's eye alone. As long as you are in a place where you are able to concentrate, you can practice this application inconspicuously anywhere and anytime.

It helps if you look at the spot you are concentrating on while you imagine with your mind's eye. Looking will help to induce the throbs or light flashes at that spot.

When your body and mind have become familiar with and adapted to this application, you may combine steps 2 through 6 with steps 7 and 8; that is, you may send inner energy up and down both legs simultaneously. You may also do the same with both arms.

1. Begin with a few *chi yi* breaths and bring on inner energy throbs in your lower abdomen.

2. Look at the top of your right leg.

3. Focus your mind's eye at the same spot at the top of your right leg.

4. Do a few more *chi yi* breaths as you concentrate on feeling a sensation at that spot on your leg. This sensation may be a throb, a warm patch, a flashing spot of light, or some other manifestation.

5. Using both your inner sight and outer sight, slowly guide this small patch of sensation down the length of your right leg to your ankle, foot, and toes. Mentally move this sensation along, down the leg, stopping every inch or so to tap that spot mentally in counts of 1-2 or 1-2-3-4. Dwell longer at the foot and toes by repeating more sequences of taps at each spot.

6. In the same way, return the sensation from your toes up to the top of your right leg (repeating step 5 in the reverse direction).

7. Now shift your inner and outer sight to the top of your left leg.

8. Focus, concentrate, and proceed as described in steps 2 through 6, applying these steps to the left leg.

9. Direct your inner energy sensation to your core. Let it pulse there for a bit. Relax, and rest for a moment.

Note: You may want to end the exercise at this point, or you may continue stimulating your arms by doing the following steps.

10. Direct your inner energy sensation from your core to the base of your neck. (If you had temporarily stopped and are now resuming this exercise, you will need to begin this step with a few *chi yi* breaths to get your inner energy going before you proceed.)

11. Place your right hand palm down in your lap. Look at the top of your right arm (at your right shoulder).

12. Focus your mind's eye at the same spot at the top of your right arm.

13. Concentrate on feeling a sensation at that spot. This sensation may be a throb, a warm patch, a flashing spot of light, or some other manifestation.

14. Using both your inner sight and outer sight, guide this small patch of sensation down the length of your right arm to your wrist, hand, and fingers. Mentally move the sensation along, down the arm, stopping every inch or so to tap that spot mentally in counts of 1-2 or 1-2-3-4. Dwell longer at the hand and fingers by repeating more sequences of taps at each spot.

15. In the same way, return the sensation to the top of your right shoulder (repeating step 14 in the reverse direction).

16. Now shift both your inner and outer sight to the top of your left arm (at your left shoulder). Place your left hand palm down in your lap.

17. Focus, concentrate, and proceed as described in steps 11 through 15, applying these steps to the left arm.

18. Roll your head in big circles, 5 times clockwise and 5 times counter-clockwise. Put both your hands over your lower abdomen.

19. Take several good stabilizing *chi yi* breaths, and relax.

Note: If you are interrupted during the course of this exercise, just take a few deep abdominal breaths to stabilize and anchor your inner energy. You may then proceed to any activity awaiting you.

APPLICATION 9

Creating a Dynamic Image

You had sufficient rest, and you are superbly dressed, yet you feel tired and drab, and you know that you look dull and project little vitality. You are on your way to a very important meeting, a photography session, an audition, an interview, or a party. You want to make an impact upon arrival. You are in your car on the way, or you are waiting for the elevator or in the reception room. You wish you could give yourself a lift. Try this application. You will feel a difference, and that difference will be visible to others.

1. Start your inner energy going by exhaling thoroughly and taking a long, deep inhalation. Imagine that you are deeply drawing in the scent of your favorite flower while also breathing through your mouth. Draw that inhalation into the very depth of you. Savor the fragrance of that inhalation for a few seconds before letting it drain out slowly.

2. Breathe in and out easily 3 times as you purposefully inflate and deflate your lower abdomen.

3. Take another long draw of fragrance, and repeat step 1.

4. Repeat steps 2 and 3 twice.

5. Your face will begin to feel warm, and your inner energy will start throbbing behind your nose and eyes. Let the throbs float through your face, your gums, the tip of your tongue, and your lips. You can almost feel a smile breaking out all over your countenance. Your face is glowing.

6. Take another long drag of air. Exhale by letting the air spill out all over.

7. You are sitting, standing, and walking tall, confident, and radiant. Keep your inner energy throbbing in your face and through your eyes as constantly as you can. You are looking great!

APPLICATION 10

Combating Insomnia

Proper breathing can be applied as if it were a tonic for insomnia First try Application 1, Promoting Relaxation. If that doesn't lull you to sleep, then capture your wandering thoughts by focusing on your abdominal breathing.

Individual sleep requirements vary; *chi yi* will not cause you to sleep naturally for much longer than your normal physical sleep requirement.

1. Breathe deeply to stimulate the core's cradle (the lower abdominal area), and to produce a throbbing sensation at the core. (Try the Tumbling Pebble Imagery Drill, page 15.)

2. Should you need additional stimulation to produce the pulsating sensation, vigorously pump your lower abdomen inward and outward 10 to 15 times, deflating as you exhale and inflating as you inhale.

3. When you have produced the throbbing sensation, focus your full attention on it.

4. As the throbbing gradually strengthens, it dominates your other sensations. Move the throbs to your thighs or toes. Imagine these throbbings as floating bubbles, *never* as bursting bubbles. Images of bursting bubbles will create an agitating effect. Notice that your breathing gradually becomes more subdued and slower, almost as though it were ebbing away. This ebbing, which produces a very calming effect, is to be encouraged.

5. When aches, pains, or discomfort are keeping you awake, extend this throbbing sensation from your core to the affected spot, allowing it to soothe and relieve the affliction.

6. Continue to monitor the throbs by counting them in repeated sequences of four, over and over. Before you realize it, you will fall asleep.

APPLICATION 11

Relieving Gas Pains in the Stomach

Gas pain is often caused by overeating or nervous tension. This application induces surges of core energy to relieve this discomfort.

Important: Be sure your symptoms are not caused by a heart condition, appendicitis, food poisoning, or any other ailment that requires the immediate attention of a physician.

1. Bring on inner energy throbbings with *chi yi* breathing.

2. Move your mind's eye to the uncomfortable spot in your stomach. Focus on that spot for a few seconds, until the throbbing begins there.

3. Monitor this throbbing for at least 50 to 100 counts.

4. You may also put your palms at the spot if your hands are warm; the warmth will encourage and intensify the throbs. You will feel rumbling at the affected area and will begin to burp and pass gas, and you will feel much better.

APPLICATION 12

Relieving Congested Nasal Passages or Sinuses

At the first hint of discomfort, do the following:

1. After you sneeze or blow your nose, concentrate on feeling a throbbing at the facial mask area and the nose.

Note: With no sneeze or nose-blowing to start the throbbing sensation, begin by focusing your mind's eye on the affected spot. Then blow your nose.

2. Pick up on the rhythm of the throbbing, and monitor it.

3. At the same time, encourage inner energy throbbings with *chi yi* breathing.

4. Continue to monitor the throbbings for at least 50 to 100 counts. You should begin to feel relief.

APPLICATION 13

Relieving Motion Sickness

At the first hint of discomfort, do the following:

1. Bring on inner energy throbbings with *chi yi* breathing.

2. Monitor your lower abdominal throbs for at least 10 to 30 seconds.

3. Focus your mind on the most uncomfortable spots in your abdomen, stomach, and throat and activate throbbings in those areas.

4. Continue monitoring these throbbings until you feel relief.

5. Breathe deeply and relax. This application may be repeated as frequently as necessary.

APPLICATION 14

Improving Speech and Singing (Vowel Production)

Each different vowel sound you produce requires a subtle variation in the way you exhale. It is important to realize the connection between such intricate adjustments of exhalation and the flow of inner energy. To some extent those adjustments are made by reflex, without any conscious effort. However, when these sounds are coordinated with selective inner energy support, you can produce each sound with a much higher degree of efficiency, which can help mend a damaged voice or add proficiency to an ordinary voice.

You use one finger to play a note on a piano. It is neither necessary nor effective to use all five fingers at once to play one note. Along this same line of reasoning, you should use your inner energy appropriately and deftly to attain the vocal production of an intended sound and to avoid clumsiness, wasted effort, or even injury.

Figures 87 through 93 show the locations of concentrated inner energy formed for producing various vowels commonly used in English and other European languages. Use these figures as a guide in helping you to direct your inner energy to the appropriate locations.

The following application will help you to achieve increased vocal proficiency. Starting with the vowel "ah" (as in "father"), visualize the image in Figure 87 as you imagine your torso to be a big hollow barrel. (Note that Figures 91 and 93 show the back of the torso.)

1. Inhale deeply to the bottom of the barrel, according to the principles of *chi yi*.

2. Open your mouth wide in preparation for producing a *hah* sound. Be sure your jaws are parted not only in front but all the way back to the jaw hinges so that the top and bottom molars are evenly parted and almost parallel.

3. Exhale with a *hah* sound, as if letting air reverberate in the empty barrel. Simultaneously imagine the shaded area in Figure 87 as air vent(s) cut out at the front of the barrel. Imagine air ventilating through these cutout(s) as you exhale in a long, sustained, aspirated, whispering *hah*. Repeat this step several times.

hah as in *father*

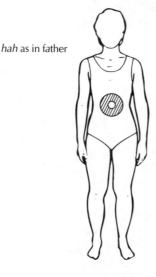

FIGURE 87

heh as in *ever*

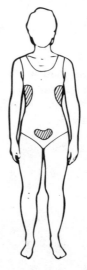

FIGURE 88

hee as in *ease*

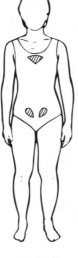

FIGURE 89

hoh as in *of*

FIGURE 90

4. Repeat steps 1 through 3, but in place of the aspirated, sustained, whispering *hah* substitute a vocal *hah*, as in regular speech. (Singers may substitute the singing of a legato *hah* at a comfortable pitch.)

hu as in would

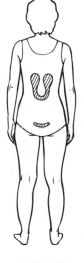

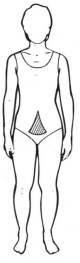

he(r) as in her

FIGURE 91

FIGURE 92

hü as in French *u* and German *ü;* combination of *ee* and *ou* sounds, with rounded lips

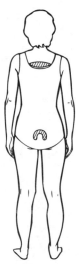

FIGURE 93

Use steps 3 and 4 to practice through all the vowels illustrated in Figures 87 through 93, one vowel at a time, being sure
to open your mouth sufficiently. Certain vowels in speech or
singing may present you with more difficulty than others, and
these problem vowels will cause a scratchy, uncomfortable sensation. If left unattended, the inefficient execution of these
vowels in everyday speech will contribute to injury and damage
to the vocal cords. Spend more time practicing these problem
sounds, being sure to use proper breath support and appropriate mouth and tongue positions. Use the figures as a guide to
the distribution of inner energy to improve your placement of
vowels and vowel production and to gradually eliminate this
vocal difficulty.

As you progress, you will be able to combine various vowels
in any sequence to gain further control and versatility in the
allocation of inner energy. Try, for instance, to say in one breath
hah—heh—hah—heh—hah—. As you produce these sounds, train
your mind's eye to visualize core energy at the locations shown
in Figures 87 and 88, alternating locations as you alternate
sounds. In the same manner, you can also try *hah—heh—hee—
hoh—hoo—he(r)—hü—*or any other combination that suits your
needs. For instance, if you have difficulty in pronouncing or
singing the word "into," practice *hee—hoo—hee—hoo—hee—hoo*
until this vowel combination is smoothed out.

By selecting a specific vowel to practice, you will isolate a
specific area of your torso to develop and strengthen.

Vowels form the backbone of speech and singing; once they
have been sturdily constructed, consonants will have a much
better chance of falling properly into place.

Simplified Vowel Exercise

The following simplified version of the previous vowel exercise may be used to help stimulate isolated areas of the torso; to emphatically activate the inner energy flow, a section at a time; and to bring on inner energy surges and throbs.

1. Breath deeply, using the principles learned in this book. Review one or more of the following imagery drills: Eyedropper, Sink and Drain, or Coil of Rope.

2. Open your mouth in preparation for producing a whispering aspirated *hah* sound. Be sure your jaws are parted not only in front but all the way to the jaw hinges, so that the top and bottom molars are almost parallel.

3. Relax your tongue and place the tongue tip behind the bottom front teeth. Exhale air sparingly, producing a sustained *hah* sound. Simultaneously visualize Figure 87, imagining that the shaded area is cut out. Imagine air ventilating through this cutout in your torso in a long, sustained, aspirated, whispering *hah* sound. As you do this several times, you will feel a slight warmth in the part of your body corresponding to the shaded area.

Use the above three steps to produce all the vowels illustrated in Figures 87 through 93 in the same whispering aspirated and sustained manner. As you produce each of these sounds, visualize the figure that corresponds to the sound you are producing. Be sure to imagine the air ventilating through the shaded areas in each figure.

All these vowel sounds may also be aspirated consecutively in one breath. For example, you may aspirate *hah—heh—hee—hoh—hu—he(r)—hü*. Or *hah—hoh—hah—hoh*. Or *hoh—hu—he(r)—hoh—hü—he(r)*.

To get the maximum benefit from this exercise, be sure to accompany each sound with the image of the figure that illustrates it. For example, if you aspirate *hoh* while imagining the air ventilating through the corresponding area at the center of your stomach (see Figure 90), the aspirating of the sound will induce inner energy to that specific area, relieving any discomfort in the stomach. An aspirated *he(r)* will not only benefit the specific area depicted in Figure 92, but will also help anchor the inhalations that follow, drawing the inhaled air to the core.

Suggestions for Using What You Have Learned

Now that you have completed the exercises, applications of *chi yi* principles, and imagery drills described in Parts Two and Three, you have built a solid, effective deep breathing system to support whatever activities you pursue. You are well on your way to achieving the major objective of *chi yi*—to derive the maximum benefit from every breath you inhale. As you continue to apply the principles of deep breathing to your everyday activities, remember that the more you practice breathing to the core, the more energy is stored and ready for use. By stimulating the core regularly and frequently with proper deep breathing, the compounded energy that you develop will improve both your mental sharpness and your physical performance.

Remember, the more you practice *chi yi*, the more adept you will become, and the easier and more natural the techniques will feel. Motivation, concentration, and persistence will pay off; as *chi yi* becomes habitual, you will gain in stamina, grace, radiance, and well-being.

All of the exercises in Part Two have been carefully planned to accomplish specific purposes. Now that you have mastered those exercises, you can put together your own program, repeating those exercises that you find especially beneficial and combining them in different sequences. If a particular imagery drill helps you with your *chi yi* breathing, use it frequently until the effect wears off, and then substitute another one—or invent one of your own.

Stay flexible in your approach, experiment sensibly, and adjust these exercises to fit your individual needs. Practice an exercise or two before engaging in your favorite sport, or whenever you feel in need of an energy boost. The investment of a few minutes a day will make an amazing difference in your overall performance.

Above all, it is my sincere hope that you will enjoy not only the actual practice of *chi yi*, but all of the physical and mental benefits it brings as well.

Questions and Answers About Chi Yi

A Dialogue about Chi Yi

Congratulations! You have reached Part Four, the question and answer section of this book, after working through the first three parts. You now have a breathing technique under your belt that will help you reach your potential in many areas of life. In Part Four, you will learn to apply this breathing technique further as you advance your powers of imagery. You will also learn to reach new heights of being in charge of your mental and physical well-being.

If you have skipped ahead to these questions and answers, you will discover fundamental information about the art of breathing as well as techniques to guide you as you develop abdominal deep breathing.

With the publication of the third edition of *The Art of Breathing* comes the opportunity for me to further explore with my readers new and more personalized ways of applying the benefits of *chi yi*. Although I have taught singing for more than three decades and conducted numerous workshops to help people refine their breathing techniques, I can't expect to meet with each of you individually. The next best option is to create a dialogue in this book through the use of questions and answers.

Teaching and learning is a two-way process. I would like to expand this process into a learning and teaching circle. Many of the questions included in Part Four have been posed by or were inspired by my students or participants at my workshops. Other queries came from readers of previous editions of this book. An answer to one of their questions may be just what you need, and it may produce a result that you have been striving for on your own.

Questions and Answers

By giving your serious consideration to the 50 questions and answers in Part Four, you will share an understanding of problems that others have experienced in their breathing practice. As a student or future teacher or healer, this sharing will give you added insight into helping yourself as well as others. The list that follows identifies each question/answer by its number and with a brief description of its content.

1. Principles of *chi yi*
2. What is *chi*?
3. *Chi* and religion
4. Is breathing a natural instinct?
5. A common mistake in breathing
6. Signs of a shallow breather
7. Are there breaks between breaths?
8. Explaining correct deep breathing
9. Explaining incorrect shoulder breathing
10. Breathing through the nose or mouth
11. Air pollution
12. Tongue tension blocks airflow
13. Dealing with gum sensitivity
14. Jaw and neck tension
15. Clearing nasal congestion
16. Physical discomforts and aging
17. Lower back pain
18. In a wheelchair
19. Emphysema
20. Asthma
21. A smoker
22. Parenting and *chi*
23. A child holds her breath

1. *Are the principles of* chi yi *as described in* The Art of Breathing *similar to* yoga, tai chi, chi kung, *or other Asian disciplines?*

Chi yi is a term I coined. Translated literally, it means *breath art* or *the art of breathing*. Anything that we learn to do well can become an art. My message is very basic: Breathe well, and other skills and benefits will follow. Without this basic skill, there can be no great performance nor can there be great health.

Think of the great breathers—superbly conditioned athletes, yogis, the Pavarottis and Streisands—who can do things that amaze and inspire their audiences. In addition to their talents and extensive skills, they have extraordinary control over their breathing.

With my bicultural and specialized training and experience, I combined techniques and concepts from both East and West to bring forth the art of breathing, or *chi yi*. *Chi yi* is a simple method of attaining a breathing technique that ensures an ample supply of both oxygen and *chi*, plus a knowledge of how to put both to good use. The art of breathing is a learned skill and does not entail any philosophy, as many ancient disciplines do. *Chi kung, tai chi, yoga,* and the martial arts are all ancient disciplines. The breathing technique you learn from *The Art of Breathing* reinforces all these great disciplines and in no way contradicts their principles.

All ancient Asian disciplines are related and are similar in their ultimate goal: the development of a person physically, mentally, and spiritually. All require the coordination of breathing with physical form. All build their principles on the subtle, all-important energy known as *chi* or *ki* or *prana*. Their emphasis and approach are what makes them different.

☐ *Tai chi* places its emphasis on results derived from disciplined body movements. *Tai chi*, sometimes known as shadow boxing, was originally created as a *chi kung* martial art. In recent decades, its primary application toward self-defense has been overshadowed, by popular demand, by its application to health.

☐ *Chi kung* places its emphasis on results derived from disciplining the mind. *Chi kung* is the discipline of *chi* energy cultivation and circulation within the body. This is accomplished through appropriate breathing, movements, and meditation.

☐ *Yoga* places emphasis on the spiritual and the philosophical, with mastery over body and mind. Acquiring the *complete breath* is a fundamental and vital part of the practice of yoga.

2. | *What is* chi?

In *chi kung* practice, the word *chi* represents the very basic vital energy of mankind and the universe. *Chi kung* teaches a healthy lifestyle, meditation, and body movements to acquire *dan tien* breathing, or breathing to and from the cradle of the core. *Dan tien* breathing results in generating and motivating *chi* to attain health and happiness.

As a classical singer and voice teacher of traditional Western music for more than three decades, I became completely immersed in diaphragmatic deep breathing, which has since become an inseparable part of my existence. The thrill of discovering the sameness of *chi kung* breathing and my singing breathing convinced me that a sound breathing technique is universal, intercultural, and timeless.

The utilization of *chi* energy is not new in the Western cultural scene. It simply never was defined and given a name. Great singers, athletes, ballet dancers, and other performers, even warriors and healers, throughout Western civilization have been using this inner vital energy to accomplish their feats.

As a performer, I am accustomed to sensing and dealing with the special inner sensation that jets my vocal sounds, the special ingredient that I employ to mold the phrases and color the tones. That special vitality helps me propel my emotion and makes me bigger than life on stage. Most performers are familiar with the existence of such an invisible and inexplicable power, but it was never labeled. I never bothered to identity it either, until I experienced the effect of *chi kung*. Suddenly I realized all those special results were produced and sustained through the power of *chi*. It is the same *chi* energy upon which traditional Chinese medicinal practices base their healing principles. When *chi* is directed externally, it enhances performance. When it is directed internally, it soothes and heals the body.

According to the principles of the *chi kung* discipline, each person goes through life sustained by a compounded *chi* consisting of two types: *prenatal chi* and *postnatal chi*. We inherit prenatal *chi*, which is also known as *original chi*, the moment we are conceived. We acquire and absorb postnatal *chi* after birth, from natural sources that include nutrients, air, and water. We reap this postnatal *chi* through disciplined living and motivated mind and body movements. This compounded inward *chi* is vital to our well-being and for sustaining all human activities. Without *chi*, a person dies.

Recent scientific research has made *chi* much easier to define. New extra-sensitive instruments are now able to sense and observe the activities of previously undetected *chi* currents. Instruments that detects infrared light are said to have picked up images of *chi* emitting from the hands of *chi kung* masters. The phenomenon of *chi* as a healing component has been well established in China for thousands of years. It may after all be taking a foothold in the science-oriented Western world.

3. *Does the principle of* chi *conflict or relate to any specific religion?*

Chi is an invisible element like the wind, the chill, or the heat. An abundance of *chi* circulating within the human body represents health, and the shortage or stagnation of it brings on sickness. The condition of our *chi* represents the condition of our internal atmosphere. The breeze, the light, and the other elements affect our external atmosphere. *Chi* is like the sunshine within, absolutely essential to our mental and physical well-being.

Chi has been recognized by the Chinese since before 2000 BC, at the time of the Yellow Emperor. Historical documentation on the phenomenon of *chi* goes back before the time of Lao Tse, who described *chi* in his *Tao Te Jing*. *Chi* cultivation and healing plays an important part in the history of Chinese culture and traditional Chinese medicine.

Chi kung is one of the ancient disciplines that evolved from the need to cultivate and harness *chi*. Since *chi kung* was a most effective way of gaining health and mental acuteness, Chinese Buddhist and Taoist monks practiced it as an aid to attaining the goals of Buddhahood and enlightenment. *Chi kung* gradually became a regular discipline in the monasteries. Simply because Buddhist monks practice *chi kung* does not mean that *chi kung* is part of Buddhism, Taoism, or any other religious or political system.

Throughout my life, I have been privileged to benefit from both Eastern and Western cultural beliefs and activities, without perceiving them as part of my religious belief. For me, ancient disciplines and traditional healings work well together with the latest vitamins and pharmaceutical pills when they are wisely combined. The idea of having to condemn or to choose, pitting one against the other, seems ludicrous and narrow minded. Why shouldn't there always be room for whatever genuinely benefits us, no matter from what corner of the world it comes? Methods of nourishing *chi* energy, or the notion of *chi* itself, are no more Buddhist oriented than taking vitamins is Christian oriented.

4. *I am accustomed to the way I breathe, and I am doing O.K. Why do I need to learn about breathing? Isn't breathing a natural instinct?*

Breathing is a natural instinct, but that doesn't mean that we naturally do it as well as we can. There is always room for improvement. Humans have learned to improve on many instinctive activities. We have learned to run faster, jump higher, sing better, and even chew more efficiently. Since breath is life, and we must breathe every moment to survive, shouldn't breathing be our most important act?

Instinctive acts are those that can just happen without our having to give them any thought. We can breathe without knowing how it happens. But suppose the time comes when we need to *make* it happen, and we don't know how. If you have ever watched someone who has difficulty breathing, or if you yourself have had to struggle for air, you know how frightening any interruption of breath can be. If you master the art of breathing, you will be better prepared to confront any health problem that challenges your ability to breathe. And when we know how to initiate and be in control of our breathing, we can then truly be capable of mastering other areas of our lives.

Breathing is our most important act because we do it every moment of our lives. How we breathe affects the well-being of every fiber in us and everything we think or feel or do. Each of us breathes an average of 20,000 times every 24 hours. If we improve just a tiny bit with each breath, think of the cumulative benefits.

When we are improperly doing other instinctive acts such as walking and talking, people around us will notice and point out our mistakes. But with the instinctive act of breathing, scarcely anyone notices how we do it. If you don't take note of how you breathe yourself, what chance do you have of avoiding the further deepening of your bad habits or mistakes? Learning about breathing and how to control it will help you take charge of yourself as a healthy human being.

5. *What is the most common mistake people make in their breathing?*

One of the most common mistakes people make is breathing shallowly. Humans are born to breathe deeply, a process sometimes referred to as *abdominal breathing*. If you watch a sleeping baby, you will notice that its stomach rises and falls with each breath. As we grow older, many of us lose this innate ability to breathe deeply, and we end up breathing into only the top portion of our lungs.

Deep breathing is inhaling into the depths of our lungs. When we breathe deeply, we breathe into the entire length of our lungs. Shallow breathing is inhaling air into only the top portion of the lungs. When we breathe shallowly, we leave the lower portion unused and therefore limit the lungs' full potential.

When we use the term *abdominal breathing* to describe deep breathing, this does not mean that inhaled air actually flows down into your abdomen. It simply indicates that you involve your abdomen when you breathe deeply, and you may get the impression that air is filling up your lower abdomen. What you are actually doing is using your abdomen to cause the lowering of your diaphragm in order to extend the capacity of your lungs. Shallow breathing is one reason you frequently hear older people complain about having trouble breathing. It is never too late to learn and improve.

An ancient adage says that partial breathing is partial living. This wisdom goes deeper than just the inhalation of sufficient oxygen. A person who breathes partially, or shallowly, throughout life never knows the pleasures and benefits of breathing deeply and misses the higher level of existence that comes from living with the abundance of both oxygen and *chi* energy. *Chi*, the inner vital energy upon which Chinese medicinal practices and martial arts are based, can be channeled to any location in the body to nourish or to heal or to soothe. This soothing effect can ease aches and discomforts, and it can lull a person to relax and sleep.

Throughout this book, you will find various imagery drills to help you experience specific sensations in the body. Doing the Eyedropper Imagery Drill on page 12 will quickly acquaint or reacquaint you with the sensation of abdominal deep breathing. You may want to take a moment to do the drill before moving on.

6. *What are the most obvious signs of a shallow breather?*

The three most obvious signs of a shallow breather are:

☐ Erroneously expanding the abdomen when exhaling and pulling in the stomach when inhaling. To breathe deeply, imagine the abdomen as a balloon. When you breathe in air, the balloon inflates, and it deflates when you blow out air. Don't worry about the fact that air never really enters the stomach. For a factual explanation, refer to the Accordion Imagery Drill on page 13.

☐ Unnecessarily lifting the shoulders when inhaling. This point will be explained in Question 9.

☐ Audibly grasping for air while talking. This point will be explained in Question 43.

You can find out more about your breathing by asking yourself the following questions. If most of the answers are yes, you need to improve the way you breathe.

☐ Does your tongue pull away from your front teeth when you take a deep breath? If so, see Question 12.

☐ Does your lower back feel rigid whether you breathe in or breathe out? If so, see Question 17.

☐ Do you clench your teeth together most of the time? In other words, do your top and bottom teeth touch all the time (when you are not talking or eating)? If so, see Question 14.

☐ Does your voice get raspy easily? If so, see Question 26.

☐ Do you feel tension in your ribcage? If so, see Question 28.

☐ Do people have a hard time hearing what you are saying? If so, see Question 40.

7. *Are there breaks between breaths?*

It depends on what you consider a break to be.

A breath consists of one inhalation and one exhalation, or one exhalation and one inhalation. Either definition is correct as the two lead into one another. Breathing can be pictured as a continuous loop of open circles, one leading into the other. They are not individual circles. You may take your time as you change from breathing up the loop to breathing down, but I wouldn't necessarily call those transitions *breaks*.

Let me compare breathing to driving a car. When you are driving forward and want to go in reverse, you put on the brakes and give yourself a bit of time to shift to reverse, but you don't turn off the engine. It's a continuous process, with pauses for changing direction. It is almost the same when you breathe, but much more eventful. As with sowing and reaping, you wouldn't want to rush the process. During our everyday activities, we instinctively know when to inhale and when to exhale. You may experience a lull but not really a break. For special-effect exercising, you may manipulate your breathing according to the special effect for which you are aiming.

Imagine in slow motion, if you will, that during a deep inhalation we draw in oxygen, and the oxygen takes care of itself. But that act of deep breathing stimulates the core, which generates *chi* energy. On exhalation, carbon dioxide is expelled. At the same time, *chi* energy is being nurtured or led to empower, enhance, or heal. Therefore, if you consider the time a breath needs to loop around and change direction to be a break, then I would say yes, there are breaks. But using the term break can be very misleading. I would prefer to call it an intentional retardando.

8. *Learning to inflate my abdomen instead of deflating it when I take a breath has helped me overcome my debilitating breathing problems. How can I explain this simply to my friends who need help as well?*

It is important to understand the function of the abdominal muscles in the act of breathing. Let's take a look at Figure 1 on page 11. Locate the diaphragm, which is the strip of muscle that separates the lung cavity from the stomach cavity. The diaphragm is the floor on which the lungs sit. The diaphragm is also the abdominal dome. This dome is manipulated by the abdominal walls, or abdominal muscles. The abdominal muscles connect with the muscles of the lower sides and lower back, forming what is referred to in this book as the *lower circumference*.

When you breathe correctly, the diaphragm lowers, allowing the lungs to elongate. Expanding the lower circumference not only elongates the lungs, this action also stretches and extends the dimension of the diaphragm. This causes the lower ribs to spread outward, expanding the lower lungs.

By doing the opposite—that is, by deflating and squeezing in your abdomen as you inhale—the abdominal muscles push the diaphragm upward. The heaving upward of the diaphragm intrudes into the lung cavities, making the lungs shorter. Eliminating the use of the lower portion of the lungs upon inhalation results in unavoidable shallow breathing.

When you breathe shallowly, you are fighting against every breath you take. As they inhale, shallow breathers pull in their stomachs, causing the diaphragm to push upward, resisting the current of inflowing air. This makes every inhalation more laborious, wasting unnecessary effort with every breath.

Refer to the Accordion Imagery Drill described on pages 13 and 14 for a visual aid that illustrates this breathing process. An additional imagery drill is effective for those who prefer more subtlety.

IMAGERY DRILL

Lotus

Imagine a large lotus blossom within your lower abdomen. As you inhale, the blossom gently and gradually opens, blossoming fully within. As you exhale, the lotus closes steadily, bringing in all its petals and becoming a bud once again.

9. *If lifting the shoulders to take a breath is incorrect and may even prevent deep breathing, how did so many of us end up having this habit?*

Throughout life, especially during childhood, we unconsciously imitate those around us—our peers, parents, teachers, and others. For many good reasons, people routinely recommend taking a big breath and then demonstrate this visually—by lifting their shoulders. Since breathing is mostly an internal act, it is difficult to act out. Shoulder-lifting, misguiding as it is, seems to be the only available gesture to suggest breathing,. You may recall a music teacher who instructed your class to take a deep breath by enthusiastically heaving his or her shoulders. Or you may remember a physician who asked you to take a big breath, lifting his or her shoulders while listening with a stethoscope. We ourselves at times may even have been responsible for unintentionally misguiding someone by lifting our shoulders to signal the taking of a breath.

When we lift our shoulders on inhalation, we simultaneously pull our diaphragm muscles upward as well. This pulls up the lower portions of our lungs, and the capacity of our lungs is greatly diminished.

When you breathe correctly, the diaphragm should lower, allowing the lungs to elongate. Lifting your shoulders has the opposite effect, raising the diaphragm just as you are initiating a breath.

Shoulder breathing presents another disadvantage. Straining your shoulders with every breath makes you a prime candidate for shoulder aches, neckaches, backaches, and other problems. Strain has a tendency to extend itself. Persistent straining often develops into chronic aches and pains and spreads to other parts of the body.

You may have observed that great classical singers, wind instrumentalists, or other "professional breathers" sometimes seem to lift their shoulders as they take a big breath. But if you observe more closely, you will notice that they first fully fill up their lungs from the bottom upward, then add more air, maximizing their lung capacity at the top as well. At such moments, they may give the impression that they are lifting their shoulders to inhale.

Refer to the Accordion Imagery Drill on pages 13 and 14 for a deeper understanding of the answer to your question.

10. *Is it more correct to breathe through the nose or the mouth?*

Most of the time we tend to breathe in and out through the nose. After all, the nose is the main entrance for breath. I generally recommend breathing through the nose—whenever it is practical and do-able—for everyday breathing.

The role of the mouth in breathing is that of a supportive portal. Sometimes it is impossible for us to breathe through the nose, so the mouth takes over. For instance, when your nose is congested with a cold, your only choice for survival is to breathe through your mouth.

Sometimes we need to take a big breath in a hurry, and breathing through the mouth and the nose simultaneously is more efficient. As you're swimming, you use only your mouth to take that big gulp of air. We tend to breathe both through our noses and our mouths when we need to catch a quick breath during conversation. Don't let ideas about breathing through the nose or mouth get in the way of what is efficient, when efficiency is vital.

You may have noticed that some breathing exercises are accompanied by specific suggestions for breathing through the nose or breathing through the mouth. These recommendations are designed only for specific results. With your everyday activities, let breathing through the nose or the mouth be a natural reflex.

The most important thing to keep in mind is the fundamental importance of abdominal deep breathing. Focusing on the nose and mouth while breathing can cause the muscles in those areas to tense up anxiously, narrowing the breathing passages. This narrowing can cause unwanted breathing noises, as if you are gasping for air. Even professional speakers and public personalities sometimes suffer from this air-sucking syndrome.

Instead of focusing your thoughts on the nose or mouth while breathing, do this: Imagine the back of the nose where it meets the throat as the opening of a funnel. Deep breathing is the key. For further details on the funnel imagery, refer to the Funnel-Balloon Imagery Drill on page 15.

11. *With air as polluted as it is, especially in many metropolitan areas, why do I want to breathe deeper and inhale more air? In fact, since I have moved to the city, I have tried to breathe as lightly as possible. I know that pollution is affecting my health. What should I do?*

Breathing involves both inhalation and exhalation. Think of the process as *exhale* and *inhale*. Compare it to emptying a container before refilling it. If you don't exhale thoroughly, you won't be capable of inhaling completely.

Knowing how to exhale thoroughly is extremely important, especially if the air you inhale is less than clean. Even if you inhale minimally in an attempt to avoid pollutants, a certain amount of air still seeps into the lower portion of your lungs. This bit of polluted air can be trapped down there for a long time if you don't know how to get rid of it.

I frequently compare this situation to little puddles of stagnant water. Foul water can breed all sorts of things. Imagine what that little pocket of stagnant air in your lungs could do to your health. Learning to be an efficient breather and using the full capacity of your lungs supplies you with more oxygen and, at the same time, assures that the air in your lungs gets thoroughly circulated.

You said that you've been breathing lightly. I presume that you mean that you're restricting yourself from breathing as you normally used to do. If you normally were a deep breather, you have now transformed yourself into a shallow breather. And if you were a shallow breather to start off with, you have now put yourself in the danger zone of health.

TARGETED EXERCISE: QUESTION 11

Air Pollution

1. Before you take your next conscious breath, sit on a chair and give your entire body several great big shakes.

2. Blow out as much air as possible by squeezing your stomach inward, pressing out every bit of air.

3. Let your abdominal muscles expand as you take in a nice deep breath, filling up your entire tank.

4. Follow with one or more thorough exhalations and inhalations, depending on your own endurance at the moment.

I think you will find these deep breaths very cleansing and exhilarating. If you feel up to it, review Exercises 1A and 1B on pages 36 and 38.

12. *Sometimes, when I consciously take a big breath to relax, my tongue seems to block the airflow at the back of my throat, and I end up feeling more tense than ever. How can I avoid this?*

I frequently refer to the tongue as the meter that measures the tension in a person's body. Take a moment to check the condition of your tongue. Is your tongue pulled back, away from your front teeth, tensed, and in a lump? If that is the case, you are not relaxed right now although you may think that you are. Somewhere in your body, tension is present.

Besides being an indicator of stress, a tensed tongue can become a roadblock that interferes with the free flow of air into your lungs. The tongue not only draws and accumulates tension, it spreads tension as well.

Tension in the tongue readily extends to the throat and vocal cords. When we speak or sing with this tension, we pass air through the vocal cords, forcing them to vibrate and produce vocal sounds when they are rigid. This rigidity is one of the causes of raspy voices and other vocal injuries. You have surely heard someone, even a child, say, "I don't want to sing anymore. It hurts my throat."

To help relieve tongue tension, try the Relaxing the Tongue Imagery Drill. The core, remember, is the center of the body, serving as a hub from which all the body's spokes draw energy and support and into which those spokes deposit pressure. When this core is well nurtured and well developed, our mental and physical balance has a pivotal point, and the world becomes less foreboding and threatening.

IMAGERY DRILL

Relaxing the Tongue

In your mind, picture the tip of your tongue. Follow it back to your throat. Imagine your tongue extending downward into your throat and further beyond, with the root ending at the pit of your stomach—the core. Bring the tip of your tongue forward to touch the back of your lower front teeth. Imagine melting the tensed lump in your mouth and letting the softening sensation flow all the way down to your core. Inhale by expanding your abdomen, and let the air drain slowly—and smoothly—downward from the tip of your tongue to the pit of your stomach. In doing so, you will breathe deeply and melt the tension throughout the rest of your body as well.

By practicing Exercise 2A on pages 46 and 47 and the Cannonball Imagery Drill on page 50, you will be able to develop greater ability to relax the tongue.

13. *My dentist and my periodontist have done all they can for me, but I am still getting frequent tooth and gum sensitivities and aches. Will using* chi *help me prevent or overcome these discomforts?*

Directing and coercing the flow of *chi* to any area in the body improves the condition in that location. Your teeth and gums are no exception. From personal experience, I find gum and tooth sensitivity not difficult to overcome with the help of *chi*, as these discomforts usually appear as throbbing pains. Welcome these throbs as challenges. Confront them by encountering each with a number. Continue to count them until the painful sensations evaporate and only soothing throbs remain. Whenever you encounter painful throbs, make certain that every breath you take puts down roots in the pit of your stomach. And as you exhale toward your gums, your breath remains anchored to your core.

We all know that overly warm or cold or sweet or sour food tends to bring on tooth sensitivity and aches. At times, we can take advantage of such a condition by initiating a throbbing episode with, say, a warm drink. Use the opportunity to bring on a current of *chi* throbs to stimulate and strengthen the condition of your gums. You may want to exercise your gums in this way when you are doing nothing much except watching TV.

See your dentist again if more complex problems reveal themselves.

14. *Whenever I am anxious or tired, my jaws start to ache, my neck muscles tense up terribly, and breathing becomes very difficult. Why is this happening? What is my problem?*

I suspect that you have a habit of clenching your teeth when you are tense. The next time pain strikes your jaws and neck, check to see if your teeth are clenched tightly together. I wouldn't be surprised if you also find that your jaws are locked and, at times, your ears may even be ringing.

When the jaws and mouth become rigid in times of stress, the tension tends to intrude into the surrounding areas. Tension travels to the back of the mouth, and the opening of the throat narrows, restraining the flow of air. Clenching causes the roof and soft palate of your mouth to stiffen. Even the nasal passages can become constricted, affecting airflow and vocal resonance. In other words, the voice may become nasal and dull. Under such conditions, it is impossible to breathe deeply.

These detrimental effects of a locked jaw are only the beginning. The tension produced by the clenching and rigidity can affect the condition of the tongue, vocal cords, the nerves in the skull, shoulder muscles, the spine, and so on. You've already noticed tension in your neck. Other problems are likely to surface if you neglect to reverse your nervous trend.

To deal with this problem effectively, I suggest you approach it simultaneously from various angles. Develop basic abdominal breathing skills. Establish core sensations. Learn to dissolve your tension down to the core. These skills need to be acquired gradually. Eventually you will be able to eliminate this chain reaction of health-threatening muscle tension.

The next time your neck tenses up, do the following targeted exercise for emergency relief.

TARGETED EXERCISE: QUESTION 14

Tension in the Jaw and Neck

1. Sit comfortably in a chair.

2. Drop your jaw.

3. Bring your hands up to cradle your chin and your lower jaw in your palms. Form a cradle by joining your wrists below your chin.

4. Gently massage your jaws with your palms and fingertips, and easily rock your cradled chin forward and backward to relax your chin and jaw. Intentionally soothe your chin and your jaw with the warmth of your palms.

5. Shift your focus to your lower stomach and lower back. Expand your abdomen as you inhale, and squeeze in your lower abdomen as you exhale.

6. To help relax your lower back and get it in tune with the expanding and squeezing, rock your body easily forward and backward and then side to side. Gently continue these rocking movements as you breathe several more times. You may notice that your lower back is participating with your abdomen in the deflating and inflating motion.

7. Drop your hands and allow them to rest in your lap.

8. Relax your shoulders by scooowing them.

9. Relax your neck by rotating your head clockwise and then counterclockwise several times.

10. Monitor the throbbings that are replacing the tension in your jaw and neck. Enjoy this healing sensation.

11. Continue to breathe deeply as you expand and compress your lower abdomen and back.

12. Imagine that all the tension is draining down, down, down...into your chair. You will find that you are breathing more deeply and easily. You should also feel much more relaxed and comfortable.

When you have a moment, take a look at the answer to Question 12. It relates to your situation as well. As you practice the exercises throughout *The Art of Breathing*, you'll want to pay special attention to Exercise 3B on page 63.

15. *My nose is frequently stopped up because of allergies.Application 12 on page 149 in Part Three of this book has helped me a great deal in relieving my stuffy nose. Are there additional approaches that I can employ unnoticed by others?*

I know what you mean. Blowing your nose at times—during a concert or a pastor's sermon, for example—is indeed disturbing. Here is another way to help bring on stimulating throbs at the nasal area to clear away the stuffiness. If your nose is stopped up as you do this exercise, it may be difficult to keep your mouth closed. However, do try to bring your upper and lower lips together, leaving some room to breathe.

TARGETED EXERCISE: QUESTION 15

Clearing a Stuffy Nose

1. Bring the tip of your tongue as far back as possible to touch your soft palate.

2. Draw a line with the tip of your tongue against the roof of your mouth, moving your tongue tip from the back of the roof and forward to touch the back of your top front teeth.

3. Repeat steps 1 and 2 five to ten times, or even more. The roof of your mouth will begin to feel warm, and you will begin to feel pulsating throbs in your nose.

4. Mentally monitor these throbs by counting them, and encourage the pulsing by breathing deeply to and from your core.

5. Count to at least 50 or 100, or more if necessary. Your nose will gradually clear up, and you will be able to breathe more freely.

It is always good to have more than one approach to dealing with a problem.

16. *Since I entered the fifth decade of my life, I usually wake up in the morning with stiff, aching fingers. I have compared notes with several of my close friends and realized that they are experiencing the same thing. We laugh and chalk up this phenomenon to aging. I wonder: Can I use* chi *in some way to ease this aging process?*

Not only will you be able to ease this specific discomfort, but you may be able to erase some of the other physical problems that come with the years.

Think of your *chi* as the inner energy being supplied by your inner battery. Each baby with normal health is born with a fully charged battery. Our individual supply of *chi* is being spent every day of our lives. The inner battery gets recharged through proper nutrition, healthy mental and physical activities such as meditation and exercise, and, above all, through the practice of abdominal deep breathing as it is taught throughout this book. When we eat, drink, exercise, and *breathe* correctly, we are able to recharge our batteries more efficiently.

During our younger days, when our *chi* is more abundant and more vibrant, *chi* circulates throughout our bodies naturally, without much intentional effort. As we grow older and our *chi* is less energized and the supply is lower, the natural effect is for *chi* flow to withdraw, first from our extremities—fingers, toes, then hands, feet, head, arms, legs, and so forth.

The tendency to misuse, abuse, and waste *chi* when we are younger leads, no doubt, to regrets as this obviously contributes to *chi* deficiency later in life. Excessive indulgence in food, sex, and unhealthy activities can dissipate *chi* rapidly. If you have not throughout the years effectively attended to the quality and quantity of your *chi* supply, begin now by making sure that you breathe correctly in such a way that you are able to generate as well as channel *chi* energy. Other activities become more beneficial when they are supported by correct deep breathing.

Chi goes wherever your mind leads it. In other words, *chi* follows your intentions. Pain and aches and even illnesses are Nature's way of turning on red lights to alert our minds to attend to the parts of our bodies that we have neglected. By turning our awareness to these red alerts, we send our *chi* energy there to heal. We can prevent illness and discomfort by being one step ahead. For instance, learn to send *chi* routinely throughout the body, especially to the extremities, before the warning red lights are ignited.

Your symptoms of aching and stiff fingers may not be your only physical complaint. Perhaps you are also getting occasional cramps in your toes, feet, and legs as well. A tired mind or a headache can also be caused by *chi* withdrawal or blockage.

Whenever you wake up in the morning and notice that your fingers and hands are stiff and aching, remain in bed for a few minutes and do this exercise:

TARGETED EXERCISE: QUESTION 16

Relieving Stiff Fingers

1. Lie on your back, with your palms facing down comfortably by your sides.

2. Relax your palms in a natural cupped position.

3. Imagine a very soft sponge in the shape of a large egg in each of your cupped hands.

4. Squeeze these sponge eggs in each hand as tightly as you can, turning your hands into tight fists.

5. Hold your fists closed for a second, then open your palms to a relaxed cup position, and allow the sponge eggs to return to their original shape.

6. Let your body remain relaxed as you breathe slowly and abdominally, as your stomach rises on inhalation and lowers on exhalation.

7. Repeat steps 4 and 5 three times, then relax. Let your palms open to a relaxed, comfortable position.

8. Notice that your hands and fingers are throbbing. If throbbing sensation is not noticeable, repeat step 7, then proceed.

9. Monitor by counting these throbs to at least 50 counts. Monitor more counts if your time allows—100 counts is a good number to reach.

10. Flex your hands by opening them wide, then closing to a fist several times.

11. Relax your hands, and notice how they are warm and full of *chi*.

12. Place your palms, if you wish, on any part of your body— thighs, abdomen, midriff, or other areas to soothe and even to heal. Enjoy yourself!

The Targeted Exercise for Question 35 (on insomnia) can also be used to lead your *chi* routinely throughout your body, including your fingers and hands. Refer also to Application 7 on page 141 in Part Three of this book, which will also lead you to find relief and even healing on your own.

17. *I frequently suffer from lower back pain. Whenever the pain occurs, I find taking a big breath almost impossible. Is there anything I can do to help myself?*

It is always a good idea to first check out a backache with a physician and get clinical tests to rule out physiological injuries. On the other hand, if no injury is diagnosed and the only prescription you get is a handful of pain killers, learning the art of breathing may be just the right thing to do.

Learning abdominal breathing according to the method advocated in this book has helped many to overcome chronic pains caused by tense muscles and lack of *chi* flow. Abdominal deep breathing not only requires that you learn to relax, expand, and compress your abdomen but that your lower circumference be involved in the same process. Because of bad breathing habits, poor posture, tension, or constant holding in of the stomach, the lower back becomes rigid or deformed, restricting not only blood circulation but also *chi* flow. *The Art of Breathing* teaches you a breathing method that does more than supply you with the oxygen that keeps your heart pumping blood through your veins. This single act of breathing must supply oxygen for survival as well as generate and circulate *chi* to ensure the quality of life and performance that all of us desire.

When we breathe, the muscles of the lower back must respond correspondingly, and their failure to do so causes rigidity, which will have a detrimental effect in that area of the body. Readers and workshop participants have informed me of surprising results from practicing the art of breathing. One reader had for years suffered periodic bouts of low back pain (sometimes referred to as *lumbosacral spasm*). He wrote me that, by virtue of practicing the exercises outlined in this book, a certain flexibility was created in that area of the back that is integral to the lower circumference, and he has become less prone to back problems.

You will find that practicing the first few exercises in Lesson 1 will yield good results. Learn to direct and apply *chi* energy to painful areas by practicing Application 7 on page 141.

18. *Can a person in a wheelchair practice the exercises in* The Art of Breathing?

Physical movements and postures included in the exercises in *The Art of Breathing* are designed to:

☐ Motivate and bring on abdominal deep breathing

☐ Relax tensions that prevent deep breathing

☐ Train the reflexes and coordinate the abdominal and diaphragm muscles

The development of other physical skills is not intentionally pursued. Even if a person is unable to move conveniently, standing up exercises can be done sitting or lying down. Stretching, bending, and other movements can also be modified to accommodate physical disabilities. The intention of almost every movement and posture throughout each exercise in the lessons is clearly explained. Understanding the intention of these movements will help you do compromised movements quite effectively.

Welcome the sensation of each bodily pain as a friendly nudge, signaling you to be aware of its location. It is Nature's way of alerting you to the need for *chi* energy at that specific area of your body. Be thankful for such sensations, and respond to them by exhaling toward that spot, letting *chi* ooze to warm, melt, and disintegrate that discomfort. Sense the pain ebb away.

Experience the indescribable sensation of mentally centering your own physical body, visiting the places where the aches are. Be there mentally to encounter and soothe whatever ails you. Treat the areas of discomfort as if they are babies, crying for attention. Guide your *chi* and make contact there, and the crying will be replaced by a sense of accomplishment.

These contacts may be in the form of pulsations, patches of warmth, or flashes of calming light. Let each sensation be like a tiny budding blossom, budding outward instead of caving inward. Let it be like a little soap bubble floating outward and blending into the atmosphere.

Imagery drills throughout the book can easily be done in a wheelchair or even in a hospital bed. In fact, during convalescence, you can have the luxury of ample free time to lavish on imagery drills. Doing imagery drills is a form of meditation that can nurture and channel your *chi* and help you gain access to your healing resources from within.

Your inner palms are always a good conveyer for exuding *chi*.

TARGETED EXERCISE: QUESTION 18

Practicing While Physically Disabled

1. Lie in bed or sit comfortably, with your shoulders relaxed.

2. Put your palms together and place them between your upper legs, or in front of you. Rub your palms against each other until they are nice and warm.

3. Place your palms against your lower abdomen.

4. Let your palms soothe your abdomen as you breathe deeply to the core.

5. Monitor the *chi* that is gradually being generated, and channel it to soothe and energize, beginning from the abdomen and moving to any other location in the body that needs healing. *Chi* is essential in helping you feel better and recover speedily.

6. Place your palms at any location to encourage *chi* flow to that point for soothing and for healing.

Not only can a person in any position do the exercises in *The Art of Breathing*, doing them is necessary to improve your condition. Every person's breathing conditions are unique, and no two people reap the exact results from any practice. Breathing exercises can be designed appropriately to accommodate specific needs.

Even a paralyzed person with an alert mind can frequently gain from employing the principles and methods of the art of breathing. For a physically able person, improving breathing efficiency can be expedited and encouraged with breath-inducive movements and postures. For a person who is immobilized, the expediting and encouraging will have to come from motivating imageries and internal stimulation. These will activate and coordinate the functions of the breathing instrument, through using the energy from within.

19. *I have emphysema, and part of my lung is gone from a cancer operation. What is in* The Art of Breathing *for me?*

Emphysema causes the walls of the air sacs of the lungs to break down. This condition, along with the lack of a portion of your lung, undoubtedly handicaps your breathing instrument. However, handicaps can frequently be compensated for, at least partially, by learning special techniques.

These breathing techniques are easy to learn. Whether handicapped or not, breathers will benefit from learning to improve the way they breathe through ably using whatever cells, muscles, and reflexes are available for the breathing process. Knowing how to handle your breathing instrument gives you the confidence of being in control.

After you have consulted with your physician and received his or her consent, the progressive exercises in *The Art of Breathing* can lead you gradually, through practice, to develop your lung capacity. You do this by learning to manipulate your diaphragm and lower circumference muscles effectively. Practicing Exercises 1A and 1B will lead you quickly into understanding this process.

Remember to do the breathing exercises without straining yourself in any way. Whenever necessary, you can adapt the exercises to your own physical endurance and condition. The number of repetitions and counts for timing indicated for each exercise in the book and video is given as general guidelines. In your situation, you may want to begin by cutting the number of repetitions and counts by half or a third, then gradually working up to your full capacity. Never force.

TARGETED EXERCISE: QUESTION 19

Emphysema

1. As a warm-up before going into the exercises, you may want to gently massage your lower abdomen. Put your palms against your lower abdomen, with your fingers pointing downward and thumbs pointing inward, almost as if you are framing your navel with your thumbs and index fingers.

2. Gently push your fingers inward, kneading from the bottom upward. Do this several times, then relax.

3. Sigh, as you feel the impulse. Good! A big sigh gives you a good start toward breathing deeply.

Now go easily into the exercises from *The Art of Breathing*. You will feel the improvement as you go along.

20. *I have suffered from asthma most of my life. While attending one of your workshops, my breathing eased up, and for the first time I felt I had a handle on my breath and that I could control it. When I got home, my wife was amazed but told me it was probably all in my head. I know it wasn't. Can you please explain what happened? By the way, I have continued to improve by practicing the exercises in your book.*

Thank you for sharing your good news with me. It is the greatest reward any teacher or author could ever ask for—that the teaching is effective in helping a special someone to improve his or her quality of life and performance.

Asthma can develop at any stage of life, in a small child or an older person. Its many underlying causes include genetic predisposition, allergies, air pollutants, stress, unnatural breathing habits, and no doubt other causes that remain to be revealed.

As of 1995, approximately 11 million Americans suffer from asthma, and it is still on the increase worldwide. Although it is not usually a fatal affliction, it can sometimes be life threatening, especially when compounded with other lung conditions such as chronic bronchitis or emphysema. Symptoms of asthma generally take the form of coughing and wheezing, chest tightness, and shortness of breath. These are signs of tightened and constricted airways and obstructed airflow.

For many sufferers, the anxiety and panic of oncoming attacks further aggravate the tightening and constricting condition. Thanks to modern science, during acute attacks, sufferers can call on powerful drugs to work near miracles, from without. But how about calling on resources from within ourselves to take steps toward prevention and even control? We can learn to reduce stress and control and manipulate our breathing instrument. Once we gain these skills, we no longer need to feel powerless. This confidence will help you relax and sidestep symptomatic episodes.

The Art of Breathing teaches you how to initiate and control a breath, not just let a breath happen. You learn to let air be drawn and not stuffed into your body. You do away with the notion (a fact) that inhaled air laboriously travels through tiny bronchial tubes and then into little air sacs and is exhaled on its round trip out through those narrow passages again. In breathing well, you need to make use of the Barrel Imagery Drill.

IMAGERY DRILL

Barrel

Imagine that your entire torso, from your shoulders to your bottom, is an empty barrel. The big opening is not your mouth, but the opening of your throat at its junction with the back of your nose. Simulate a yawn with your mouth closed, and you'll find that opening. Be sure not to block that opening by pulling back your tongue (see information about the tongue on page 45). Let inflowing air coming through the nose or the mouth or both flow like water into the bottom of this barrel. As you exhale, imagine that this water flows out by way of a drain at the bottom of the barrel.

Contrary to common misinformation, asthmatic attacks frequently affect exhalations more than inhalations. You may be able to breathe in air, but when you breathe out, constricted and inflamed airways may collapse, causing exhalation to be extremely laborious. Making use of the Barrel Imagery Drill helps negate the sensation of breathing air desperately through constricted passages and helps relax muscular tension and relieve emotional anxiety.

Refer also to the Steam Funnel Imagery Drill on page 123 and the Sink and Drain Imagery Drill on page 125. The imagery drills are helpful in supporting the actual breathing techniques that you will acquire as you practice the exercises in Part Two of this book. Learn to let your diaphragm lower by expanding your lower circumference (lower abdomen, lower back, and sides), allowing air to flow in effortlessly. Refer to the Accordion Imagery Drill on page 13.

If you rely solely on the movements of your shoulders and ribcage to pump in air, these over-worked areas will become tense, causing the air passages in the vicinity to tense as well. This avoidable tension may bring on spasms of the airway muscles and contribute to asthma attacks. Learn to let your diaphragm and abdomen assume the workload of breathing as Nature intended.

Breathing abdominally shifts the mental focus of breathing from the lung cavity to the abdominal cavity, allowing the lung cavity and all that is within it, including the bronchial tubes, to be more relaxed and healthier.

Asthma sufferers need to beware of vigorous physical exercise, yet regular workouts are beneficial. The exercises in this book are moderate yet subtly effective. However, always be watchful not to overexert yourself, especially on days when conditions are conducive to asthma episodes; that is, when the air you breathe in is very cold or very hot or when the pollen count is high. Remain aware of your own physical endurance on a given day, and adjust the duration of the exercises accordingly.

The points brought out in the response to Question 19 (about emphysema) are also relevant to asthma.

21. *I am a smoker. After playing tennis, if I take a puff on my cigarette right away, I feel like it burns my lungs. Why is this? Is it more harmful to smoke right after tennis?*

Likely you have not been a long-time or regular smoker. If you had been, the inside of your lungs would be more thoroughly coated so that a single tennis game could not have bared the tender spot that the burning sensation made noticeable. You would have been much more desensitized.

During vigorous exercising such as playing tennis, you breathe deeper and more frequently, and your lungs are, more than usual, stretched and flushed with fresh air. Compare the situation to applying something that stings on the grimy skin surface of your face; you may not feel the sting at all. Scrub your face clean, and your skin will be more likely to react to the stinging substance.

I have never been a smoker. I often wonder if part of the satisfaction of taking a big puff on the cigarette is due to the act of taking a deeper breath. The cigarette works as a prop for inhaling deeper than the smoker otherwise would. Take away the cigarette and the smoker is left with no apparent reason for the conscious drawing in of air. Little shallow breaths seem good enough for mere survival. How depressing! Not only the withdrawal from nicotine but the withdrawal from the act of a deeper breath brings on the unbearable withdrawal symptoms.

The Art of Breathing should be very helpful to those who sincerely want to quit smoking.

22. *Can a mother's shallow breathing habit affect her baby or her young children?*

The role of a mother can be as demanding as any professional career, or even more so if you take into account that it is an around-the-clock demand of both physical energy and emotional attention. A mother's good or inferior mental and physical health is reflected onto her young children. All this goes for a father, too, under the same full-time situation.

To breathe deeply, a mother replenishes her *chi* and imparts it to the baby in her arms or the child in her lap. The child feels contented and thrives. On the contrary, a shallow-breathing mother, usually short of *chi* , unconsciously saps *chi* from her baby or child. Anyone who is *chi*-deprived tends to sap *chi* from whomever is closest. Both health and disposition are affected by the way we breathe. Have you ever wondered why a baby sometimes cuddles contentedly in one person's arms and cries in another's, although both are either strangers or family members? *Chi* is not the only reason, but it is one of the reasons.

Crying is only part of the negative effect of depleted *chi*. When a mother breathes shallowly, usually by heaving her shoulders, her child unconsciously imitates her and becomes a shallow breather as well. Breathing habits are reflected in the speaking voice. Have you ever wondered why all the children in a family have similar nasal or squeaky voices?

A mother possessing an ample supply of *chi* can be a healer for her child. She cannot take the place of a physician, when a physician is called for. But a healing mother can soothe, calm, and melt away minor discomforts as no medicine can. This contributes dramatically to a child's physical and emotional well-being. For instance, a mother's *chi* exuding through her palms can penetrate deeply to help a colicky baby. Stroking the back of a baby as he or she cuddles in your arms basking in your *chi* produces great healing effect. Stabilizing deep breathing creates a stabilizing atmosphere in a home. All this effectiveness relies on your ability to breath effectively.

One evening, I visited someone whose baby was struggling to get over a cold. The baby was cranky and wriggling in her mother's arms. I placed my palm over the baby's back and, in a short moment, the baby's whining changed to gentle coos. She turned around and gave me a great big smile and cooed some more as I maintained my palm on her back. I was told the next day that the baby slept well that night and was back to her normal chirpy self.

23. *My eight-year-old daughter is very sensitive to my quick temper. If I show anger to anyone in the household during the evening, she sporadically holds her breath and sometimes vomits in her sleep. How can I remedy this tension before sending her to bed?*

Your daughter's holding her breath can cause her to vomit in her sleep. She holds her breath by steeling her ribcage and her diaphragm muscles, which in turn causes her abdomen to contract. You can clearly imagine the chain reaction that is set in motion. It is absolutely unhealthy to put her to bed in that condition.

Yours is a situation that seems to be beyond the realm of breathing. Its emotional complexity suggests a need for professional psychological assistance. However, if you want first to try to remedy the situation on your own, here is my suggestion.

Whenever you have a temper flare-up and are able to simmer down and realize the upcoming consequences for your daughter, ask for her help before she goes to bed. Tell her that your anger has made your breathing difficult and shallow, and you want her to help you do some breathing exercises. Make her feel needed. Bring out your book or video and do the beginning exercises in *The Art of Breathing*, with both of you monitoring and helping each other with abdominal inflation and deflation as you breathe deeply and thoroughly. Place your palms on each other's abdomens, backs, and sides as you give suggestions to each other about the workout. Make this workout serious yet playful. This is a wonderful way to loosen up and warm up to each other, as well as help yourselves breathe deeply. Don't be surprised if acquiring a deep-breathing technique enables you even to control and dissipate the anger that arouses your temper in the first place.

Whether you decide to take on remedying your situation on your own or to consult a psychotherapist, learning to breathe more efficiently will play an important part in the healing process.

24. *My daughter lost her hearing when she was two years old as a result of meningitis. She is now eight and attending a specialized school for hearing-impaired children. How can I equip myself to help her speak?*

Instinctively, we learn to speak by imitating what we hear, without bothering to understand the intricate process of voicing—that is, how a voice is produced.

For a person deprived of the sense of hearing, learning to speak becomes an extremely laborious process that requires admirable intelligence, diligence, and tenacity. When a sound is vocalized, the monitoring of the end result of that vocal sound through hearing must be replaced by attention to other values such as muscular sensations, vibrations of resonance, and other measures.

As the human voice is basically a wind instrument, it depends on exhaled breath to flow past the vocal cords in order to produce a sound. Therefore, learning a proper breathing skill greatly enhances and facilitates the acquiring of an effective speaking or singing voice. For a hearing-impaired person, acquiring the ability to control and manipulate breath effectively is the single most important step toward learning to speak successfully.

I presume your daughter must be receiving correct breathing instruction in school to help her along with her voicing. You can certainly help her by being able to breathe appropriately. At all times, especially when she cuddles up to you, she observes and feels how you breathe. If you are a shallow breather, she will consciously or unconsciously imitate your breathing habit. A bad breathing habit is the last thing she needs on her uphill road toward learning to form vocal sounds without distortion. As you learn the art of breathing, you will become more sensitive to her needs. Your ability to pass the skill on to her will undoubtedly influence her success.

25. *I am a dental hygienist. I have been told that neckaches and shoulder aches come with the profession. I didn't believe that five years ago, but now I know these discomforts firsthand. I would like to believe that I can ease or even counteract this so-called occupational hazard. What do you suggest?*

Leaning forward to peer into patients' mouths is indeed a very unnatural posture to be stuck with most of your working hours. Compounding the constant lifting of your arms, reaching into your patients' mouths and working delicately with your fingers is no easy feat for any physical body to endure. The demands of this extremely unnatural posture—stretching and bending your neck and even your upper back—cause your spine to go out of alignment. As you lift your arms and control your finger movements, all that control and strain backs up into your shoulders. Shoulder stress is passed on to your neck, your upper spine, and downward toward your feet.

Your distorted posture definitely affects your breathing as well. In your situation, you cannot count on instinct to take care of your breathing. You need to apply the abdominal deep-breathing technique to strengthen your core and to establish a well-grounded center within your body.

Your working posture lends you to shallow breathing. The constant lifting of your shoulders draws up your diaphragm muscles as well as the lower portion of your lungs, preventing you from breathing deeply. You must develop a definite skill in controlling your breathing by using your lower abdomen, lower back, and sides. Pay special attention to the exercises in Lesson Four beginning on page 77.

Learning abdominal deep breathing will help you establish a pivot point at the core for your physical bearing. Consider the roots of a tree. A deep-rooted tree provides its trunk, branches, and even leaves with deep-rooted support and strength. The stress of the branches is passed on to the trunk and downward to the well-grounded roots.

A human body needs to establish such a grounding as well, in order to draw strength from the core and pass stress downward to be absorbed by the core. With a strong core to pivot upon, you can balance your body parts upon it, instead of aimlessly grasping for support and ending up with stressed out, aching body parts. Breathe to the core. Draw strength from the core, and balance at the core.

The Breathing Tree Imagery Drill will help you relax muscular strain due to undesirable working postures.

IMAGERY DRILL

Breathing Tree

Imagine your body as a tree, standing alone in the wilderness. You are a big tree with a big sturdy trunk, numerous branches, and luscious leaves, reaching upward toward the sky and outward toward the surrounding atmosphere. Plant your feet a few inches apart and firmly on—seemingly *in*—the ground. Bend your knees slightly.

Place your palms against your lower abdomen, and monitor your breathing. Deflate your abdomen as you exhale, and inflate as you inhale. Do this several times. Then let your hands fall easily to your sides. Continue to breathe to and from your abdomen.

A breeze approaches and all your leaves rustle and your branches wave gently. Feel all your body joints relaxing, and let your body parts relax and move with the breeze. Let your shoulders seesaw and rotate freely. Let your arms, hands, and fingers flow freely like the branches and leaves of a willow tree.

A stronger breeze approaches, and the branches and leaves move more distinctly. The top of the tree (your head) sways easily in any or all directions—backwards, forward, sideways, and even in rotation—as your feelings lead. Let your neck and shoulders respond to the movements. Connect the movements to your upper spine and gradually down the spinal column to your tailbone. Now imagine that the tree has a flexible trunk, like a birch, that blows in the wind. Imagine a tail extending from your tailbone. Sway your tailbone and swish your tail in any direction your mind suggests. Let your hips, knees, and ankle joints relax and cooperate with your swaying movements.

Be certain that you are breathing abdominally. Inflate as you inhale, and deflate as you exhale. You may even imagine that the entire tree is inhaling and exhaling through its very pores. This is very important. Not breathing this way will leave you without the support of your core, and ultimately without the continuous generating and circulating of *chi* energy throughout your body, and unable to take full advantage of this imagery drill.

At first, do the imagery drill for a minute or so to see how your body adjusts to this regimen. You can increase the duration according to your own physical endurance and needs.

26. *I am a classroom teacher. I must speak in a loud voice in many of my classes, and my voice gets raspy very easily. Are there any breathing exercises that will help me with this problem?*

I've been asked this question many times. In fact, anyone with insufficient *breath support* eventually has this problem. Raspiness is an issue in particular for people such as school teachers and lawyers who speak to groups for a living. And it frequently happens to others as well who make presentations for fun at social gatherings.

Our lungs envelop our breath, and the diaphragm is a strip of muscle that supports the lungs. When a person knows how to manipulate the diaphragm so as to control the flow of air in and out of the lungs—at any desired speed and force—we can consider that as having breath support. The degree of control can be learned.

Abdominal deep breathing not only gets oxygen into the lungs, it also stimulates the core to generate the inner bioenergy known as *chi*. This inner vitality not only makes us healthier but also makes us more capable and efficient in every way, and that includes the delivery of your voice.

Think of the voice box as a wind instrument. You need to control the air that passes through and vibrates the vocal cords to produce specific sounds—high or low, soft or loud. Our minds, in cooperation with our hearing, know exactly what sounds we want to make. If our diaphragm is not capable of controlling the flow of air, the throat and tongue muscles assist by tensing, causing the vocal cords to tense as well.

In this way, even though the desired vocal sounds may be produced, the vocal cords are forced to vibrate while they are in a rigid state. The vocal cords become injured, and the voice begins to sound raspy. In extreme cases, nodes may develop on the vocal cords, necessitating surgery. Like a raspy voice, constantly having to clear phlegm from your throat is another red light cautioning you to take heed that you may be abusing your vocal cords.

To make a long story short, breath is voice; breath is life. To gain breath support, you need to make use of your diaphragm. To use your diaphragm efficiently, you need to cultivate abdominal deep breathing by practicing at least the exercises in Lesson 1. After that, you will most likely find the incentive to develop your breathing skills further. Please refer back to Question 12 for additional insight.

27. *I have been told that I am stiff and expressionless when I make presentations at our office meetings. I've tried to include some body movements and gestures in my talks, but my body just doesn't respond. I feel that if I move any muscle, I will fall apart. Could this be a breath-related problem?*

Yes, your stiffness is likely related to the way you breathe. I believe that the culprit behind your problem is shallow breathing.

People who breathe shallowly tend to compensate by using their shoulders as a lever to pump in needed air. The habit of lifting the shoulders strains the shoulder and neck muscles and builds tension in the spine, causing stiff, uneasy movement.

Shallow breathers also have difficulty centering their bodies, resulting in inferior physical coordination. Putting feelings into movements or speech requires that you be in touch with your core and its energy. Shallow breathers are often cut off from their dynamic energy source.

Developing abdominal deep breathing not only relieves body tension, it goes a step further. The constant expanding and compressing of the abdomen generates *chi* energy. By stimulating the core with each breath and developing awareness of its existence, you are continuously nurturing a center within your total being. This center can become a stabilizer for your mental and physical coordination.

The next time you make a presentation, imagine that you are inhaling all the way to the pit of your stomach and exhaling all the way through your toes and fingertips. I think you'll find that you are standing more steadily, and that your hands and body are more willing to help you express your thoughts.

Besides practicing the breathing exercises in the beginning lessons, I suggest that you also practice Application 3 on page 133 and Application 9 on page 146. These applications will help you further improve both your speaking abilities and your body language.

28. *For several years, I've worked as a salesperson standing behind a cosmetic counter most of the day. I've gradually developed a gripping sensation all the way around my rib cage. No matter what I do, the discomfort around my ribcage still persists—in fact, it's getting worse. I can't even breathe comfortably. I feel breathless most of the time. What should I do?*

Throughout civilization, for both men and women, conforming to the dictates of fashion has been uncomfortable at times, and it can even be injurious to your health when carried to an extreme. Remember the historical days of waist cinching and foot binding? In your case, presumably, wearing tight-fitting clothes and standing behind a stylish counter—almost on display—can turn your flexible body into a rigid statue.

I can fully understand, for I once had a similar experience with a job in sales. Decades ago, when I was a college student, I took on part-time work in a department store during the Christmas season. I stood behind the jewelry counter, all spruced up. In those days, that definitely included spiked heels and dresses that were form-fitting—especially tight around the waist.

I was inexperienced, and I was nervous, which made the job seem even more exhausting. At that time, I couldn't understand why the job had affected my singing. I knew it was affecting my breathing, and I worked hard to counteract that compressed sensation around my ribcage.

Fashion has impressed upon us that our abdomens and back ends should disappear at all cost. Top-heavy is the mode. The bottom half of the torso, containing the vital organs within, has become permanently held in and rigid. We lose our natural ability to breathe abdominally, and we develop all sorts of problems, including back pain, a rigid ribcage, and shallow breathing.

To help you relieve your discomfort, here is a simple exercise. You can do it while standing, sitting, or lying down.

TARGETED EXERCISE: QUESTION 28

Body Tension

1. Place your left palm against your left ribcage, and your right palm against your right ribcage.

2. Massage by rubbing both sides firmly and deeply in a rotating circle—clockwise for the right side and counter-clockwise for the left. Let your shoulders rotate with the flow to avoid tension buildup there. The stretching and kneading helps relax tense muscles in this entire area. Do this approximately 10-15 times, loosening the tensed muscles and relaxing the ribs.

3. Reverse the massage rotation, rubbing clockwise on the right and counter-clockwise on the left. Do this 10-15 times. Let your shoulders move with the flow.

4. Leave your palms where they are and shift your attention to your lower abdomen. Mentally, monitor the inflating of your abdomen as you inhale and the deflating as you exhale. You will begin to feel the warm *chi* energy exuding

from your palms penetrating into your ribcage, soothing and melting away the discomfort.

5. Dwell on and encourage this wonderful sensation as you lower your hands relaxingly to your sides. Gradually extend and spread this warm, perhaps even pulsing, sensation down toward your lower abdomen and up toward your shoulders and neck.

6. As your whole torso gradually warms up, rotate your neck and shoulders simultaneously, gently loosening your spine by rotating and twisting your torso.

Lessons 1 and 4 are especially helpful for loosening the ribcage muscles. I suggest that you also take special note of Exercise 2D on page 56 and Exercise 4B on page 83. I recommend going through the lessons in this book progressively, according to the numbers, to gain maximum long-lasting results.

29. *I am a licensed massage therapist. My best friend is a nurse who also practices therapeutic touch. Our work drains a lot of energy from us. Will improving our breathing help our endurance?*

Body workers such as you and your friend share a great amount of your *chi* energy with your patients as you work on them. Patients tend to have blocked or imbalanced energy flow as well as deficiencies in their *chi* supply.

Anxiety, stress, tension, and injuries, among other reasons, cause minute, invisible entities to take form in our bodies. For lack of a better word, I call these entities *knots*.

A healthy baby should be born with a clean slate. But if, for example, a pregnant mother is on drugs, in an accident, or encounters emotional traumas or other mishaps, invisible knots may be imprinted onto her baby's slate. Somewhere along the way in this baby's life, the knots will surface as mental or physical conditions that need to be dealt with.

Throughout life we all experience stress, trauma, and injuries. All these experiences create invisible knots.

Many adults may feel that they have dealt with whatever emotional or physical crises they have experienced and have put them behind. But knots may still loom up to confront a person in the future as various forms of mental and physical complications. Knots in any form block the flow of *chi* energy and can cause aches, pains, discomfort, and illness.

Chi energy, that vital force upon which many ancient Asian healing arts are based, is the life force that influences our blood flow, our very cells, and our vibrancy. Through constant revitalization of our *chi* energy with proper deep breathing, vital *chi* can be channeled to overcome and clear up blockages that are caused by knots.

As body workers, when you are consciously manipulating, modulating, or even jump-starting human energy, you must be certain that you are consistently able to recharge your own pertinent level of *chi*. When your energy is low, a patient's negative current may overpower your defenses, and you may sometimes end up with your patient's physical problems. *Chi kung* practitioners are especially careful to make certain that they are able to fend for themselves in order to be helpful to others.

Abdominal deep breathing stimulates the core and generates human *chi* energy. Deep breathing skill enables you to meditate effectively, allowing you to manipulate and channel *chi* efficiently. As you work, whether or not you come into actual contact with your patient as you massage or employ therapeutic touch, be certain that your mindful healing intention flows *as you exhale deeply*. Maintain a magnetizing consciousness at the core—not gripping but easy and glowing. It's not advisable to heal others when you are exhausted.

Once in New York City I accompanied a friend on a visit to a well-known *chi kung* master who uses massage and acupuncture for healing. His method is to direct his *chi* energy through his hands as well as conduct *chi* through the acupuncture needles to maximize the healing effect. He had been unavailable for several months, and my friend asked him why. He shared his unfortunate experience with us. A first-time patient came with a pain in his leg that had persisted for several years with no apparent physical reason. The man's appointment came toward the end of a grueling day, and the master was tired. His *chi* was at a low level, and he positioned himself carelessly as he did the work. The next day, he ended up with the same leg pain as his patient. It took him months to rid himself of that negative current.

Yes, breathing effectively is one of the most important prerequisites for engagement in conscious participation of the healing process of another.

30. *My work schedule is extremely intense, and every day I must meet deadline after deadline. Recently, I noticed, much to my alarm, that I had stopped breathing momentarily. I was really surprised—and frightened. What is happening to me? Why does my breathing stop? What can I do about it?*

It can be very frightening to feel that you are not breathing, even if it's only for short moments. It comes as a shock because people tend to think of breathing as something that happens automatically. We're used to just breathing. But when your mind has been taken over by an intense workload, your natural reflexes become desensitized, and your breathing becomes so shallow that you can barely feel it.

Momentary loss of your breathing sensation can also happen when your lungs are congested during a flu attack. You lie in bed, already feeling miserable, when suddenly your lungs just seem to go on strike. That's when you realize that you can't take your next breath for granted.

If your breath seems to fade off again, revitalize it by speaking a few words in a loud voice. You can make a short remark to someone or just talk to yourself. If you're alone, you could just say, "No, no, no, no, no. . . " until you have emptied all the residual air from your lungs. In this way, Nature will then take care of you by making sure that your next breath is going to be big and deep. Follow your vocal outburst with several more deep breaths. Your face will probably feel flushed and your body may even be tingling. Your breathing should bounce into good form.

If you know the song "Oh, What a Beautiful Morning," you could sing it at that point. It has a such an exhilarating message. You could sing any song that comes to mind. "Don't Worry, Be Happy" is another good choice. Just a short verse is good enough, but you may want to sing more. Singing is therapeutic. It's a way of awakening both your body and your mind with conscious breathing. Learn to maintain this deep breathing by practicing the exercises in Part Two of this book.

Yes, breathing usually does "just happen," but doesn't it make sense to understanding the process and to know what you should do if your breathing hesitates? Learn the art of breathing, and each breath will take on a new meaning—forever. Bolstered with new breathing skills, you will know that you are in charge of your body's most important function. In touch with the breathing process, you will probably stop experiencing involuntary lulls in your breathing. And if it ever happens again, your deeper understanding will allow you to take action.

31. *I have been working very hard all my life and never could find time for physical exercise. When I retired recently, I made a resolution to take better care of my health through exercising. In spite of my plans, no exercise I've tried seems to work. I am always out of breath after the first few minutes. I begin to feel that my lungs are filled to capacity and there's no way I can suck in more air. Can learning the art of breathing help me?*

Yes, learning the art of breathing can help to provide an increased oxygen supply and improve your ability to regulate your breath appropriately. What you are experiencing is the result of years of poor breathing habits. Gaining higher levels of breathing skill should not be difficult if you set your mind to it and approach the process step by step.

Specifically, what you are experiencing is, in part, a consequence of shallow breathing. Right now, you are probably using only the top portion of your lungs. This handicapping of the breath occurs through the misuse of the diaphragm—lifting your diaphragm on inhalation instead of lowering it to allow more air to flow into your lungs.

This simple exercise will give you a good start on breathing deeply. It is a good one, too, to do before getting started on any of your physical training sessions.

TARGETED EXERCISE: QUESTION 31

Out of Breath

1. Stand with your hands dangling by your sides.

2. Exhale as you raise your arms to the side to shoulder height, keeping them straight.

3. Inhale as you lower your arms to their original position. (The simple movements in steps 1 through 3 will help reverse the unwanted tendency to lift the shoulders when inhaling. After practicing the steps a few times, focus your attention on deflating the abdomen on exhalation and inflating the abdomen on inhalation. Once you have accomplished that, go on to step 4 and complete the exercise.)

4. Again, exhale as you raise your arms to shoulder height.

5. Inhale by lifting your hands up toward the sky, reaching high, and breathing deeply into the pit of your stomach.

6. Exhale as you lower your arms to their original position by your sides, and deflate your abdomen. Inhale deeply.

7. Repeat steps 4 through 6 several times to encourage deep breathing.

Practicing the exercises laid out in this book will lead you to correct these mistakes and whatever other adverse breathing habits you may have acquired throughout your life. It will guide you in applying, with ease, proper breathing technique to your daily activities. The art of breathing supports and enhances any form of exercise—aerobics, cycling, tennis, golf, swimming, and others.

32. *I love sports. I jog, play tennis, and have recently picked up golf. I also swim and ski when the opportunities arise. However, recently I have on occasion felt out of breath. I went for a physical checkup with my physician and was assured that nothing is clinically wrong with me. My friend tells me that better breathing will improve both my athletic skills and my energy level. How should I approach this task of better breathing?*

Feeling out of breath is a sign of shallow breathing. You are using only the top portion of your lungs. Under the physical stress of exercise, the top portion of your lungs is overstrained. The bottom portion, which remains undeveloped, is unable to share the workload intended for your lungs at full capacity.

Learn abdominal deep breathing by developing your ability to manipulate your abdominal and diaphragm muscles. Expanding your abdomen on inhalation and compressing it on exhalation causes the lowering of the diaphragm and facilitates the drawing in of air into the lower portion of your lungs.

When you breathe deeply, you will be much better equipped to facilitate activities of varying intensity, from the most strenuous to the very gentle. Your natural instinct will initiate "big" deep breaths to sustain the more demanding activities and "small" deep breaths to maintain peaceful, relaxing moments.

As we inhale and exhale deeply, two things happen simultaneously: the lungs receive ample oxygen and expel carbon dioxide, and the abdomen expands and compresses, creating the inner energy that the Chinese call *chi*. That is, every time the abdomen inflates and deflates as you inhale and exhale, the core at the center of the abdomen is stimulated and *chi* energy is produced.

Chi, when directed internally, improves health and promotes healing. Externally, this energy, directed by the mind, works as a combined steering wheel, accelerator, and brake. *Chi* improves coordination, one of the main requirements for attaining athletic skill. No one can perform anything great on inhaled air alone. *Chi* must accompany any superb performance.

Abdominal deep breathing that stimulates the core also nurtures a core center within us. This cradle of the core develops and establishes a pivot point within our bodies upon which our physical and mental activities are stabilized and do not flounder. All well-executed physical movements are initiated from this center, propelled by *chi* energy targeted for best results.

Acquiring a sound deep breathing technique takes discipline and practice, especially at the start. Practicing the progressive lessons in this book along with *The Art of Breathing* companion video can make the learning process more expedient and enjoyable. Practice leads to a breathing ability capable of supplying ample oxygen and generating significant *chi* energy to keep you well-centered and in the best of form. You will then be able to carry out, with flying colors, any mental or physical activities you wish to undertake.

33. *Can mental tensions be relieved with proper breathing? I ask this because whenever I am caught in traffic, I get agitated and then I start to feel a knot or lump in my chest. It used to happen only when I was late for an appointment, but now it seems that I feel this knot whenever there is a traffic jam.. I keep telling myself that reacting this way is going to give me a heart attack someday. Can improving the way I breathe help me get rid of this uncomfortable sensation?*

When we're stressed and in tight situations, we tend to tense our diaphragms, producing that gripping sensation. When the diaphragm shortens and stiffens, breathing becomes extremely shallow. During a traffic jam, we're confined to the car with no route of escape. As our hands grip the steering wheel, our anxiety is compounded by the pressures of time. "There's no way I'll make that meeting now," you groan silently to yourself. So what do we do? We tighten our muscles. The entire body becomes a great big knot, and the chest becomes the center of that knot.

Yes, you definitely need some breathing skills to loosen that knot and melt the tension. You cannot get up and walk around nor can you bend or stretch during a traffic jam. I suggest you experiment with the Melting Tension Imagery Drill. Be sure to stay alert and pay attention to your driving.

Melting Tension

Sit forward slightly, leaving a little room between your back and the back of the seat.

Shake your body from side to side, from the shoulders down to your bottom. Let your torso, especially your abdomen, shake like a bowl of Jello. Do this for a few seconds, loosening your joints and muscles.

Pump your stomach in and out several times to flex the muscles in that area.

Loosen your tight grip on the steering wheel, making sure that you are still in full control of your steering.

Blow out air as you pull in your stomach, and breathe in as you inflate your stomach. Let your stomach react like a balloon, inflate with air, and deflate without. Do this several times.

Relax, and bring your attention to the uncomfortable tightness in your chest. Imagine it to be a chunk of frozen ice cream of your favorite flavor.

As you breathe out by squeezing your abdomen, and breathe in by expanding your abdomen, allow the flowing warm air to loosen and melt the cold chunk of ice cream.

Let the melted ice cream drip down deeply into the pit of your stomach, saturating it. Shake your body and loosen your spine gently to help with the flow.

After a few minutes of this imagery drill, you will feel more relaxed. The lump will be melted and you may feel like smiling. You may even want to hum or sing your favorite song. You may find that you are singing better than ever after using your newly acquired, simple, deep-breathing ability.

34. *Many times I feel the need to give my lungs a thorough cleansing, especially after I've been sitting in a traffic jam, breathing in exhaust fumes, on the way home.*

It really is a good idea to sweep every corner of the lungs once in a while. It doesn't have to be only after encountering polluted air; anytime you feel stuffy or stale is a good time for refreshing your air tank. Before you do the targeted exercise, turn to pages 152 and 153 and familiarize yourself with the figures and their accompanying open vowel sounds.

Every combination of vowels and consonants, when voiced, affects different parts of the body, especially the lungs, in its own special way. To be produced, each sound requires a specific combination of cell and nerve efforts. Going into details on this topic requires a whole new book. But at this time, let me suggest the following exercise for some results.

It is extremely important that you do not overexert yourself with this exercise. You can stop at any step and continue after rest intervals.

TARGETED EXERCISE: QUESTION 34

Cleansing the Lungs

1. Sit, or lie down on your back, with your arms resting comfortably at your sides.

2. Say *pah—teh—pah—teh* . . . with a snatch of breath between each sound. Explode (pop out) each sound by pulling in your lower abdomen. Snatch in an inhalation between sounds by expanding your abdomen. Follow this pattern: *pah* (inhale)—*teh* (inhale)—*pah* (inhale)—*teh* (inhale). Expand your abdomen with each inhalation. This process is very simple. We will refer to these two staccato syllables as *the handle*. The above sample represents two handles strung together. Practice the handle by repeating it several times.

3. Inhale, then voice the handle followed by *tah—tah—tah—tah—tah—tah—tah—tah—tah—tah*. Flex your stomach muscle in, then out with each *tah*, without taking any breath. Do 11 to 15 *tahs* until you are out of breath. We will refer to this sound series as the *a* vowel whip. As you voice the handle (*pah—teh*) followed by an *a* vowel whip (*tah—tah—tah*...), visualize the location of the cutout in Figure 87. Consult the pronunciation guide that accompanies Figure 87. Rest for a few seconds, and breathe freely. As you continue, refer to the accompanying pronunciation

guides for each figure. Add the explosive consonant "t" to all the vowels to make a whip.

4. Inhale, then voice the handle followed by the *e* vowel whip (*teh—teh—teh...*), as you visualize the location of the cutout in Figure 88. In this step, you will notice the repeat of *teh* between handle and whip. This is correct.

5. Inhale, then voice the handle followed by the *i* vowel whip (*tee—tee—tee...*), as you visualize Figure 89.

6. Inhale, then voice the handle followed by the *o* vowel whip (*toh—toh—toh...*), as you visualize Figure 90.

7. Inhale, then voice the handle followed by the *u* vowel whip, as you visualize Figure 91.

8. Inhale, then voice the handle followed by the *huh* vowel whip, as you visualize Figure 92.

9. Inhale, then voice the handle followed by the *hu* vowel whip, as you visualize Figure 93.

10. Breathe deeply, and relax! Place your palms over your abdomen as you monitor your pulsing energy throbs. After the initial minute or so of monitoring, feel free to let your palms move to other areas of your body. Let your instinct guide you to the spots where your palms will give the most comfort and soothing.

It is good if you have the time to rest and nap a bit after this exercise, which is also effective in helping you to sleep or go back to sleep when you're wakeful during the night. Experiment with it.

35. *Going to sleep at night has been my biggest problem for many years. I have tried various ways including counting sheep, and nothing seems to work. Whenever I have important morning appointments, I sometimes grudgingly resort to sleeping pills and tranquilizers. I have been told that perhaps learning to improve the way I breathe may ease this problem. Is there any chance?*

Tension, mental or physical, is one of the main causes of insomnia. Another is a wandering mind that refuses to be turned off. A more stressful cause is physical pain or discomfort.

The art of breathing enables a person to handle an ample supply of oxygen, generate *chi* energy, and nurture a mental and physical core. Each helps relieve insomnia.

Breathing incorrectly definitely interferes with sleep. The act of breathing can itself cause tension if you do not understand and possess the skill of easily drawing in and expelling ample air out of the lungs. Raising your shoulders as you breathe while you are lying in bed causes restlessness. Sucking in air without knowing how to make room for the inflow restricts the flow. Forcing the lungs to extend downward without the help of the diaphragm and the abdominal muscles is impossible.

When we are resting, we do not need big deep breaths. Gentle little deep breaths are much more appropriate and quieting. With your palms on your lower abdomen, gently inflate your abdomen as you inhale, and deflate as you exhale. As you do that, the whole act of breathing falls into place, and it becomes natural, effective, and relaxing. If you want to sleep like a baby, learn to breathe like a baby—breathe abdominally.

As you breathe with your abdomen, expanding and compressing, the area and the vital organs within are being gently massaged, relieving the tension you have unintentionally accumulated.

This expanding and compressing also stimulates the *dan tien*, or cradle of the core, and *chi* energy is generated. *Chi* is the inner vital energy (bioelectricity) upon which Chinese medicinal practices and martial arts are based. There are various catagories of these ancient disciplines. The stillness *chi kung*, frequently known as meditation *chi kung*, is the discipline of using your mind to direct the flow of energy within your body. As your mind motivates *chi*, unwanted thoughts flee, and you fall asleep.

Practice Application 10 on page 147. Sometimes just simply placing your palms against your lower abdomen and feeling the warm *chi* penetrating inward is sufficient to soothe you to sleep.

You may also want to try the Journey of the Three Strings Imagery Drill the next time you have trouble sleeping.

IMAGERY DRILL

Journey of the Three Strings

Before you attempt this, you must be able to breathe abdominally or it won't work. During the course of this imagery drill, you may at times feel that your breathing has switched to a slow-motion mode, and you may even feel that your breath has suspended. This is Nature's way of quieting down your breathing in order for your visualization to come through more clearly. You may fall asleep before the end of the journey, and that is perfectly all right. If you wake up in the middle of the night, you can resume the journey where you left off or postpone it to another time and start from the beginning if you wish. Be prepared for unusual, surprising sensations along the way. Beneficial chain reactions at unrelated locations in the body are not unusual. One night, as my mind was traveling down the back of my legs, my nose suddenly cleared up. I was unaware of that minor nose blockage until I had the comparison of total clearing.

The Journey of the Three Strings Imagery Drill can be done at any time and in any position—standing, sitting, or lying down—as a soothing and healing regimen. It is a wonderful way of getting acquainted with your inner body and learning how your mind can lead your *chi*. I find it most effective in helping me relax and sleep. When you are tired and it is time to sleep, this regimen can work like magic. It may look foreboding, but it's simple once you begin.

Lie in bed and imagine three strings, each starting from the top of your head. Split the first string so that you draw it on both sides, symmetrically, from the top of your head down to the spot on your head above your ears (make a stop, and pause for two slow counts at *each* stop). Continue downward along the sides of your neck to where it turns toward your shoulders (stop). Lead toward the tops of your shoulders (stop), downward toward your elbows (stop), your wrists (stop), and to your fingertips (stop).

Go back to the top of your head and lead the second string down the center of your face (stop at the point between your eyebrows). Stop next at the tip of your nose. Move the string to the center of your lips (stop), to the tip of your chin (stop), and then to the dimple at the bottom of your neck (stop). Continue inching downward easily, as if you were mentally blowing soap bubbles and counting them at each stop to propel you to move another inch toward the next stop. Gently blow one bubble at each stop as you mentally travel down the front center line of your body toward the pubic bone. Split the string into two, and lead the two symmetrically toward each hip joint {stop). Continue inching downward and stopping, reaching the knees (stop), the ankles (stop), and the tips of your toes (stop).

Go back to the top of your head and pick up the tip of the third string. Lead it down the back of your head. Stop at the center back of your head, then move to the nape of the neck (stop). Now inch gently down the center of your back, stopping at each inch, in the same manner as you did down the front. Inch toward the tailbone (stop), and split the string into two, symmetrically, inching and stopping down the legs toward the heels and forward along the center of your feet. Dwell somewhat longer at the arches. Inch forward toward the bottom of your toes, stopping at each toe. Still monitoring your toes, add the top of your head and your core into the picture in your mind. Your entire body is now saturated with *chi* energy. Stay calm and relax. Breathe gently and deeply as if all the pores throughout your body were breathing.

Now bring your attention to focus and gather your *chi* at the core. Then relax.

---

36. *My mother, who is 70, fell and broke her hip. She was in the hospital for several weeks and is now convalescing at home. Should I introduce her to* chi, *or should she simply rest and do the prescribed physical therapy three times a week?*

Seventy years old is still an active age for most people to pursue the power of *chi*. Only recently have I learned from a distinguished Chinese herbal doctor of a general guideline not to overextend the application of *chi* to patients above the age of 88 or 90, taking into consideration that everybody ages differently. His principle is that when a person reaches a certain age, *chi* should be allowed to ebb and take its own course without external *chi* stimulants such as potent herbal tonic and acupuncture.

Moreover, a sufficient amount of prenatal *chi* needs to be present in order for a body to accept externally induced *chi* effectively. As a rule, the prenatal *chi* of the very old is usually rather spent. Untimely external *chi* stimulation for the very elderly may intrude upon the natural flow that plays an important part at the very late stage of life. *Chi* generated by deep breathing, *chi kung*, *tai chi*, yoga, or any other self-discipline is beneficial for people of all ages as these are not considered unnatural externally-induced *chi*.

Many people believe that the best way to feel better is to ignore an illness or pretend that all is well. I strongly believe, on the contrary, that a sick person does much better by acknowledging and participating in the healing process, if at all possible. If the discomfort or pain is overwhelming, seeking relief from medicinal pain killers may be necessary. However, to be threatened by and unconditionally surrender to pain and discomfort is to undermine and waste the power of *chi*, which is our most precious natural endowment. Physical pain and suffering can loom over us, or we can loom over them—with weapon in hand. Frequently, we have a choice. Keeping our weapons in working order is the wisest act for self-confidence and preservation. Begin by making sure that we breathe effectively, breathe the way we were born to, before distortion took place and turned us into shallow breathers.

If I were your mother and had never been introduced to the self-help aspect of *chi* healing, I would be extremely grateful to be guided toward a new dimension of self-care through this ancient wisdom of healing.

---

37. *Applying perfume has always been a good way for me to get my second wind after a long day. It's not just that I enjoy smelling good. The fragrance actually revitalizes me. Is there a substantial reason for this?*

A wonderful smell, whether coming from food or perfume, always makes us take a prolonged whiff or two. It instinctively makes us want to take the biggest, deepest breath we know how to take as we savor the pleasure.

Yes, your perfume inspires you to inhale more deeply, increasing your oxygen intake and waking up your sleepy cells.

Beautiful scent gives you an emotional lift, especially when things around you seem tiring and dull.

The next time you want to maximize the benefits of smelling, imagine the fragrance coming from a distance.

Distant Fragrance

Focus your sight on something at a distance. Imagine, for instance, that you are smelling the fragrance from the blossoms outside the window in your neighbor's garden or on the treetop on the distant hill. The farther away the sighted object from which you can draw your smelling inspiration, the deeper your inhalation will reach into your body. Imagine that distant scent is being drawn magnetically to the pit of your stomach, where it takes root. This imagery drill will increase both your oxygen and your *chi* supply.

Developing the skill of abdominal deep breathing can help you benefit more fully from aromatherapy, the practice of using fragrances to relieve stress and tension and to create a desired state of mind.

38. *Can the exercises in* The Art of Breathing *replace the physical exercises I am now doing?*

The exercises in this book are not intended to substitute for your other physical exercises. These exercises are designed to build a sound breathing technique that supports and reinforces all your other activities. They teach you to make the most out of every breath you take in order to establish a firm foundation upon which every aspect of effective living can be built. Learning the basic technique of breathing is like learning the English or Russian alphabet before you learn to speak the language or the stroke components of Chinese or Japanese characters before you learn to write. Once you know the basics well, you are much better equipped to learn to speak or write a language, and once you have built deep breathing skills, you are better prepared for all the activities of life.

I am sure you remember countless times when you were reminded by various people to take a deep breath to improve whatever you were doing. It could have been:

☐ Your tennis coach

☐ Your gym teacher

☐ Your aerobics instructor

☐ Your ski coach

☐ Your cycling partner

☐ Your doctor

☐ Your psychotherapist

☐ Your herbalist

☐ Your voice teacher

☐ Your band leader

☐ Your drama coach

☐ Your yoga master

☐ Your meditation instructor

☐ Your painting teacher

☐ Your scout master

☐ Your mother

☐ Your father

The list can go on and on.

Did any of the people who made this suggestion to you ever take the time and effort to make sure that you were complying correctly with their request? Did you at the time even know how to take a deep breath? "Take a deep breath" is a great and convenient remedy for overcoming all sorts of physical and emotional hurdles. But for something as important as "a deep breath," it is wise to make sure that you know how to take one.

Although breathing exercises can't replace physical activity, your physical exercise needs to be accompanied by correct breathing. Without it, you may even hurt yourself.

39. *Does* The Art of Breathing *help with centering oneself physically and mentally?*

Absolutely! The benefit of practicing the art of breathing is threefold. You gain:

☐ The ability to breathe in ample oxygen for quality health

☐ The ability to generate, cultivate, and channel *chi* for personal power and healing

☐ The opportunity to cultivate and nurture a pivotal center (the core) for physical and mental stability

Let's just do a recap on the first two points, then get to the third, which deals with your question.

☐ *Oxygen.* In order to breathe in more air, the diaphragm must lower on inhalation to allow the lungs to elongate, creating air space. The muscles of the lower abdomen, lower back, and sides, which constitute the lower circumference, must expand to cause the diaphragm to move downward. The expanding of the lower circumference also expands the lower ribcage, broadening the lower portion of the lungs. In other words, in the correct scenario, the lower portion of the lungs not only elongates but also expands, creating more space to hold ample air.

☐ *Chi.* As the lower circumference expands and compresses with every deep abdominal breath, the core in the center is stimulated, creating a force within. This is the inner vitality that manipulates and propels intricate, exacting, and dynamic outward physical expressions, movements, and vocal sounds. This is also the *chi* energy that Asian medicinal principles and martial arts are based upon.

☐ *Core.* Consider your core to be the hub of a wheel. You are the wheel. All the spokes reach outward from the hub and draw their support from this center. Breathing to the core nurtures this center. We can further cultivate this center by constantly being aware of its existence and its vital role as the hub from which we draw the energy to motivate all our physical activities, and to which we deposit unwanted tension. Refer to the section "The Core" on page 9 for more detail.

To center yourself physically, you must perceive all you do as being connected to and extending from your core. Your movements are motivated, coordinated, and energized from this center. When all your activities originate from this center, you will feel stabilized, under control, and centered. Look, for example, at the act of sitting down. You can do it so much more easily and gracefully by simply imagining placing your core into a chair. Forget about struggling with the 100- or 200-pound bag of a floppy body. To stand up, just imagine lightly picking up your core. When you are centered, you are much more able to be in full control of your body and your movements.

All mental activities should be securely anchored and skillfully manipulated at the central core. I have used the imagery of flying a kite elsewhere in this book to demonstrate other functions. The kite analogy explains so well the effectiveness of remote control.

IMAGERY DRILL

Remote Control

Center yourself mentally by imagining all your mental activities as kites that have their strings held at the core. You can simultaneously fly many kites as long as your center is cultivated enough to handle them. Let the able kites fly high and reel in any that stray.

40. *People tell me frequently that they can't hear me speak, although I am talking as loudly as I can. Can I learn to speak louder by improving the way I breathe?*

Absolutely, yes! The response to Question 10 offers some information about how to do that, but let me elaborate. You need to gain breath support by developing abdominal deep breathing.

We are each born with a voice. That doesn't necessarily mean that we know how to put it to good use. Let's compare the voice to a musical wind instrument, such as a trumpet, a clarinet, or a saxophone, which must be blown into to create music. Without air passing through our vocal cords, there can be no sound. Without breath support, there can be no strength in the voice.

The voice is the most complex of all instruments. It's built in. We can't see or touch it. We produce sounds by imitating what we hear. When a person is born without the ability to hear, making effective use of his or her vocal instrument is quite challenging and sometimes impossible.

Not only do we need breath to make a vocal sound, the amount and intensity of that breath flow determines the volume and quality of that sound. We can increase the volume of the voice by learning to inhale deeply and to empower the breath with core energy. By focusing the voice, we increase its ability to jet forward and be carried afar. It's like throwing a snowball. If it's not packed together, it won't travel very far. We can improve the carrying power of the voice by learning to control the diaphragm effectively.

Learning to control and manipulate our breathing instrument—and the core—will help us convert the air we inhale into a jet stream and propel vocal sounds toward our listeners. It is amazing how a very soft *pianissimo* musical sound made by a great singer or a flautist can carry to the last row of a concert hall.

Whereas singing emphasizes vowels, speaking emphasizes consonants. Improving your diction by enunciating the consonants more clearly and vividly allows others to hear you better. Consonants are the arrows of speech. They will help you deliver your message.

Refer to the Cannonball Imagery Drill on page 50 to understand the basic principles of jetting a vocal sound with abdominal deep breathing.

---

41. *I am extremely shy, especially with strangers. I come off as being very quiet, but deep down inside, I really would like to talk more. I have much to say! I worry about my voice quavering, and at times I even stutter slightly, and when people can't hear me and ask me to repeat, I wish I could crawl into a hole and disappear. Will improving my breathing help me with this social problem?*

Suggesting that you "take a deep breath" would seem a ridiculous oversimplification of your dilemma, and you may have heard that suggestion many times before. And yet your shallow breathing is the root of your predicament.

Taking a deep breath is effective only if you know how to do it correctly. Shallow breathing uproots your stabilizing center and causes you to feel unsteady, physically and emotionally. Uncertainty causes you to fumble, which blows your self-confidence. Combine that with your lack of breath support, which is also due to shallow breathing, and your voice becomes inaudible and quavering. Trying to steady your voice sometimes brings on stuttering.

Answers to a number of questions in this part of the book will help you understand your situation more clearly and give you insight as to its causes. Practicing some of the exercises in Part Two will help correct your shallow breathing habit. Your center will be nurtured and strengthened, your speaking voice will improve, and your shyness will gradually evaporate as *chi* takes over.

42. *Both my wife and I are in our seventies. During this past year or so, my wife has gradually been talking less and less, and recently she has almost stopped talking. She says that she can hardly breathe in enough air to survive, let alone have any left for speaking. We have been to doctors and therapists. We have been told that there is nothing wrong with her lungs or her vocal cords. She needs to breathe better. Can you help her?*

It's never too late to improve on the way we breathe. True, habits are hard to change, but a great deal of improvement can be accomplished at any age. A great way to begin is by gaining an understanding of how the changes can help.

Your wife has been using only the top portion of her lungs for many years. Many people unknowingly end up breathing this way. That overburdened top portion of her lungs eventually became overexerted and exhausted.

Imagine using only one of your two arms. Wouldn't the unused arm become limp and useless? As we grow older, our lung muscles, like our other muscles, lose some of their elasticity and resilience. Eventually, even the accustomed, inferior way of breathing degenerates further. The top portion of the lungs is strained from being overburdened for years, and the bottom portion is undeveloped from neglect. The diaphragm, which has never been put to proper use, has become unresponsive. This is why many older people end up with breathing problems, which will also affect their voices and speaking ability.

In efficient breathing, most of the work is done by the diaphragm with the support of the abdominal muscles. Shallow breathers, on the contrary, allow the diaphragm to heave upward by squeezing in the abdomen on inhalation reversing the natural function of the diaphragm.

Your wife should first reacquaint herself with the reflexes of the muscles involved in the breathing process. Here's an exercise for her to start off with.

TARGETED EXERCISE: QUESTION 42

Speech and Aging

1. Put your palms against your lower abdomen, and massage it deeply but gently, bringing circulation and sensation back to this area.

2. Blow little puffs of air through your mouth as your abdomen pumps in and out. Pull in as you blow, and expand as you take in a quick wisp of air. In doing so, you cause the diaphragm muscles to move up and down, loosening tension in the abdomen and enlivening its sensations.

After this initial reawakening of the dormant muscles that are crucial for breathing, your wife will be more prepared to proceed with the practices of Lesson 1 in this book. As she progresses, Exercises 2B on page 50 and 4C on page 86 will help her reconnect breathing with the important explosive consonants of speech. This will lead her toward breathing more effectively and speaking with breath support.

Speaking of support, your taking the time to ask this question indicates the great concern you have for your wife's predicament. Give her all the support and encouragement she needs to accomplish the goal you share: that she will soon be able to talk clearly and happily.

43. *I recently listened to a tape of my voice, and I was quite surprised that I could hear every breath I took. These gasping sounds were really quite annoying, yet I never before realized that I make them. Can doing the exercises in* The Art of Breathing *help me breathe more quietly?*

Yes, developing abdominal deep breathing allows you to breathe in without tensing and constricting your throat, nostrils, and other air passages, which causes air to squeeze in rather than flow in freely. Right now, you are partially compensating for your lack of breath support by tensing—and thus narrowing—the throat and nostrils. When you do this, your inhalation sounds rushed and noisy.

How you inhale depends a lot on how you exhale. When you learn to exhale deeply, you'll be able to inhale deeply and easily. Imagine that exhaling thoroughly is like squeezing a rubber ball (your abdomen): the harder you squeeze the ball, the faster it springs back into shape.

Like exhaling and inhaling, speech and breath are interdependent. While you are talking, the act of speaking replaces exhalation. If you don't inhale deeply, your next sentence will not carry well. And if your voice trails off at the end of a phrase, your next inhalation will be shallow and even gaspy. Experiment. You can also try breaking up a sentence with breaths between every word. Soon you'll find yourself gasping for air.

A good speaker, like a good singer, must learn to breathe effectively. This takes practice. With time, you will find that deep breathing strengthens your diaphragm muscles. A well-developed diaphragm provides the breath control that you are now lacking. Once you have that control, you will be able to manipulate your inhalation with ease. Your throat and nasal openings will remain relaxed as you inhale, allowing air to flow in rapidly—and quietly.

The exercises in Part Two of this book will be of particular interest to you and to others with similar problems. By practicing the exercises in this book, you will eventually eliminate those gasping noises.

For a fast reference, turn to page 44. The answer to Question 26 contains other insights that may help you breathe more quietly.

44. *Recently I started taking lessons in ballroom dancing. My instructor keeps telling me that I slouch and gives me tips for improving my dancing stance. But when I try to hold up my head, my back end sticks out. And when I pull in my back end, I can't breathe freely. It seems that my posture is affecting the way I breathe. Is this possible?*

Yes, posture and breathing do closely affect each other. A good relaxed posture represents a more receptive container into which air can flow deeply. When you can inhale deeply into your lower abdomen, you'll have more energy and a better sense of centering. This will naturally lead you to better posture. The effects of improper handling in one area or the other can bounce back and forth between the two, building and compounding your problem. Since posture's effect on breathing is probably more obvious to you, we'll work first on that issue. Practice the following exercise to improve your problem gradually

TARGETED EXERCISE: QUESTION 44

Posture

1. Stand in front of a mirror, preferably one that's floor length. Look at yourself straight on in the mirror.

2. Turn your head easily from left to right as far as you can, three times in each direction. End with your head looking forward.

3. Place your palms against your lower abdomen, and monitor your breathing. Deflate your abdomen as you exhale, and inflate as you inhale. Take three deep breaths. Return to casual breathing, with your hands to the sides.

4. Lift your shoulders, one side at a time, as high as possible while lowering the other, without straining, and seesaw them 10 times. When you've finished, stop and rest, with your shoulders in their regular position.

5. Return your palms to monitor the breath, as in step 3.

6. Swing your hips from side to side, as far as you can without straining, while slightly bending the opposite knee. Do 10 full swings with your hips, five to the right and five to the left, as you dangle your hands comfortably by your sides.

7. Return your palms to your abdomen and monitor your breathing as in step 3.

8. Imagine that you have a long hanging tail that is an extension of your tailbone. With your palms against your lower abdomen, monitor your body as you lift your pubic bone forward (up) by tucking your tail under. Swish your imaginary tail forward and backward 10 times, as you lift and lower your pubic bone. Rest for a moment.

9. Return your palms to the lower abdomen, and monitor your breathing.

10. Walk around the room and continue to breathe deeply as you swish your tail, sweeping easily and gracefully, forward and backward, left to right, by bending the opposite knee. Hum a dance tune and do your favorite steps with freedom in all your joints and with your head facing the center and forward. No more slouching!

Practicing some of the breathing exercises in Part Two, especially the one for posture, will further help you improve. Refer to the String of Beads Imagery Drill on page 31.

45. *Our choir director constantly reminds us to take big breaths. Is a big breath the same as a deep breath?*

Big breaths and *small breaths* seem to be self-explanatory terms. But a big breath does not necessarily contain a good supply of air unless the breath is inhaled deeply. *Deep breathing* is inhaling to fill up the entire lungs, top portion as well as bottom portion. *Shallow breathing* is inhaling air into only the top portion of the lungs, leaving the lower portion unused and thereby limiting the full potential of the lungs. Shallow breaths, whether big or small, are limited breaths. Deep breaths of any size are valuable. All deep breaths have their moments of effectiveness. Big deep breaths are perfect for strenuous activities such as running and exercising. Small deep breaths are suitable for resting or sleeping. The various ranges of activities require various sizes of deep breathing, and our instinct coordinates our needs for us. In breathing, deep is the important factor.

To initiate a deep breath, you must lower the diaphragm muscles by expanding the abdomen. That is why the terms *abdominal deep breathing* and *diaphragmatic deep breathing* are interchangeable.

Refer to the Accordion Imagery Drill on page 13, which will help you visualize the connection between your lungs, abdomen, and diaphragm.

46. *I am a singer, and I plan to be a professional performer. I have been told, and I know, that I have a beautiful voice. However, my nervousness overshadows my voice whenever I am on stage, and I feel very discouraged. Will learning the art of breathing help me overcome my extreme stage fright?*

A certain degree of nervousness or anxiety is frequently helpful in bringing off a great performance. It activates the adrenaline factor. It helps to bring one's attention into sharp focus and moves a performer into high gear, physically and mentally. Being overly nervous can be a hindrance. Several other factors are absolutely essential for a successful performing singer. The analysis that follows may produce a clue as to the cause of your extreme stage fright.

A singer must be in full control of his or her vocal instrument, and a sound breathing technique is a vital foundation. As a singer you do not need me to tell you that. You must already have realized the intricacy of what voice training is all about: breathing, resonance, placement, focus, volume, coloring, agility, vowel and consonant formation, phrasing, and much more. Still, I think I can help you discriminate between a sound breathing technique and a not-so-sound one. Without a sound technique, a singer will be unable to score well on what he or she wants to achieve. A sound breathing technique emphasizes breath support and is careful with breath strength. A breath that you can anchor on and manipulate is far superior to one that pushes or forces out a seemingly big voice. A singer's breath can caress or torment his or her voice, determining whether or not that voice will last. Sufficient vocal and breathing technique gives you more confidence and reduces nervousness.

A singer must consider a breath to be much more than the air that has been inhaled. The magical skill of lacing this air with *chi* has been demonstrated by great singers and other performers for centuries. Amazingly, Western culture has had no name for this magic. Asian cultures have labeled this internal, energizing, vibrant element *chi* or *ki* or *prana*, for self-empowerment and healing. A singer who has the skill to generate and harness *chi* through abdominal deep breathing has a much better chance at success. Without *chi*, breath support or vocal technique for artistic vocal deliverance is limited. So many singers employ *chi* to embellish their careers. Yet they do not recognize nor have a name for their benefactor. Employing a magic wand consciously instead of unconsciously can be much more masterful. Cultivating an abundance of *chi* helps reduce tension and nervousness.

Let's go backwards with this reasoning process. Without *chi*, breath support is limited. Without good breath support, the vocal instrument cannot be fully under control. Without having the confidence of controlling the vocal instrument, the singer feels insecure and has good reason to be nervous.

A singer must *thoroughly* learn and know the music to be performed. The scariest thing is to forget what comes next during a performance. Practice until you are able to pick up a song at any phrase. Have the first word of every phrase or verse pegged securely in your mind. Melodies usually stream along, but when you stumble on a word, the melody and the beat can get thrown off. An experienced piano accompanist can rescue you when you stumble, but with an orchestra, wow! Not knowing the music well enough can add greatly to the stage fright of any performer. One of the worst nightmares for a singer is forgetfulness in the midst of a performance.

Some people are more predisposed to stage fright than others, and not necessarily entirely because of the factors we've discussed. Experience gradually helps you discover specific ways to prepare yourself. In the meantime, you will find that the exercises and applications suggested in this book will help you gain much control over your breathing, *chi* manipulation, stage presence, and self-confidence. Attaining this mastery will make a difference when you get on that stage.

47. *I used to play in our university band even though I was a liberal arts student. Playing the trumpet gave me so much enjoyment, but I had to give it up because of my academic workload and, later on, my professional demands. Now that my career and my family life are on a good course, I have taken up trumpet playing again. I am taking lessons, but somehow my breathing is falling short of the demand. Do I need to do breathing exercises, or will more practice on the trumpet accomplish the same thing?*

Why take the long tedious road when you have a much more direct way to go? You have already wisely identified the cause that limits your ability to play well. Take care of the problem as proficiently as you can. Practice appropriate breathing exercises.

As you probably know well, playing the trumpet isn't just forcefully blowing air through the instrument. Intricate techniques are involved, and the most essential of these is breath control. Like singing or playing any other wind instrument, the breath you inhale not only needs to be abundant, but it also needs to be manipulated and energized. Without establishing this basic foundation, your playing will be compromised.

I am very grateful to one of my readers, a professional trumpet player, who wrote to tell me that practicing the exercises in this book helped make his tones bigger and fuller with less effort, through a wider range of both pitch and dynamics. Such wonderful news!

48. *A great big laugh always helps me feel so much better physically and mentally. Life is not full of great big laughs. Is there any way I can duplicate this good feeling in some other manner? Is there a certain way of breathing that will produce the same effect?*

I love this question! It brings back the memory of my rehearsals for the performance of Gian Carlo Menotti's one-act comic operetta *The Telephone*. Lucy and Ben were the only two characters. Lucy, the airhead heroine, talks (sings) a blue streak of beautiful melodies, interjected with shrieks of laughter from one conversation after another over the phone. Ben wants to propose to Lucy in person, but he is frustrated by the endless ringing of the phone. He ends up proposing over the phone instead. It was such great fun for me to learn how to put on a hysterical laugh and giggle impressively at any time between phrases of singing. I am sure I drove everyone in the house up the wall with my laughing practice.

Yes, laughing is thorough exhalation, bringing on instantaneous, deep, thorough inhalation. What a wonderful way to bring on deep breathing. You can almost get high on such jubilation. When something is funny, you can't help but laugh, which is Nature's way of letting you release that overwhelming emotion. However, it is also workable to put the cart before the horse—that is, to use abdominal breathing to propel laughter, from giggle to belly laugh.

IMAGERY DRILL

Funny Spot

Focus your mind on the spot about an inch or two above your pubic bone. I call that my funny spot. Flex that muscle in and out a few times and vigorously blow out a few puffs of breath as you think "happy" and smile. Mentally, still focusing on the funny spot, bounce off a few giggles from the depths, then laugh out loud. Imagine that the funny spot is fluttering in and out. Your laughter will take off like a kite, but be sure that the string is attached securely to your core. Laughing is quite contagious. You will have a whole roomful of people laughing with you just because you are laughing.

Laughing, singing, sighing are all very effective ways of getting a good emotional and physical workout. Breathe deeply and stay centered and grounded to avoid any possible emotional and physical "dip" after a big laughing episode.

Laughing is the best medicine for any ill. Laugh, and the world laughs with you!

49. *On certain days, my mind tends to feel spaced out and groggy. On such days, when I am confronted with an imminent important meeting, presentation, or interview, I wish I knew a fast pick-me-up breathing formula that would wake up my mind as well as my body. Is there such an exercise?*

Are you referring to those days when you are overworked and underslept? Or to days when you should be physically fit but are not feeling up to par?

I propose an exercise that quickly alerts both your body and your mind and even puts a shine into your eyes, provided you have not been unreasonably overtaxing your mental and physical capacity and health. That is, you have been taking care of yourself, but you still feel the need for a pick-me-up. This formula is workable only if you have already learned how to breathe abdominally.

You can do this exercise as a daily morning routine, before breakfast, if you wish. It should keep you wide awake for several hours, so don't do it near bedtime.

TARGETED EXERCISE: QUESTION 49

An Expedient Pick-Me-Up

1. Stand with your feet parted, perhaps a couple of inches wider than shoulder width, with your toes pointing slightly outward.

2. Dangle your hands freely at your sides. Inhale deeply through your nose, and exhale thoroughly by blowing through your mouth.

3. Inhale deeply again, then exhale slowly as you arch and bend forward as far down as you can without straining, but not much more than a 90-degree angle.

4. Continue to exhale as you move your hands to cup over your knees and spread your elbows as though they were wings. Continue to exhale slowly.

5. Stand up gradually to original standing position and place your hands on your waist. Exhale all air.

6. Inhale slowly and deeply, expanding your abdomen.

7. Bend your knees outward over your toes as you dip your body downward, in a saddle position (as shown in Figure 62 but with your hands on your waist). Further inhale an additional portion of air as you dip. Hold your breath and straighten your knees, bringing your body back to standing position.

8. Dip and further inhale, adding another portion of air to the bottom of your lungs. Hold your breath and straighten your knees as you stand back up. Dip down as you inhale; hold your breath as you bob up.

9. Repeat step 7 several times until you feel that the lower portion of your lungs is fully stretched and filled with a maximum amount of air. Note: Steps 5 through 8 may look complicated on paper, but they total only a few seconds once you put them into action.

10. Stand up and exhale thoroughly from your core as you lower your relaxed hands to your sides. Capture the sensation of your exhaled air (*chi*) spreading to the top of your head, exuding through your wide-open eyes as they gaze far yonder, and spreading throughout your entire body, including your fingers and toes.

11. Breathe deeply and fully for a few seconds as you monitor the soothing throbs that are defogging and opening your mind. *Breathing deeply* throughout is a must. Even as you exhale, the breath must still be anchored at the pit of the stomach.

12. Repeat the above 11 steps one or two more times but no more than that. Be a good judge of your own endurance. Wait until the next session for more repetitions. Don't do more than two sessions a day.

50. *Nancy Zi, do you, the author, regularly do the exercises in your book* The Art of Breathing? *Do we have to practice these exercises as a long-term routine?*

Learning the art of breathing is like learning to ride a bike. Once you know how to do it, it's with you for life. However, only *perfect* practice makes perfect. Once you get the hang of it, be sure to practice applying deep breathing to everything you do. Refer to the exercises in the book and video periodically to make sure that you stay on track and continue to improve. Eventually, for me, abdominal deep breathing became a second instinct. No matter what I am doing—exercising, walking, driving, working, and even relaxing, deep breathing is with me continuously. If I were to try to breathe shallowly, I would have to make an effort.

"Thoughts on Lesson 6" on page 119 will give you suggestions for maintaining what you have learned without long-term repetitive exercising. You can always diversify or structure your own special routine—one that you enjoy living by and can share with others to let them know what you have discovered along the way. Creativity has no limit once the fundamental techniques are mastered.

Epilogue

As I advance in my inner and outer disciplines, I have developed a sense that my body consists of two forms: the *vital* form and the *grounded* form. I trust that some of my readers, particularly those who are highly refined in their mental and physical discipline, have had similar perceptions. What is my vital form? What is my grounded form? How do they come together, and how do they work separately? How does the *yin* and *yang* balance of the vital form compete with the gender features of the grounded form?

Getting on with aging has been a fascinating process for me. Each new day allows me to move another step toward something new. Like a magical lotus flower, I find myself graced with yet another petal at every turn. I open a little every day and discover new rays of light.

I work diligently at counteracting, or at least retarding, the aging process of my physical body with personalized exercise programs, good nutrition, and the avoidance of unhealthy activities and excessive indulgence. Above all, my abdominal deep breathing habit—the one that you have just learned from the work laid out in Part Two of this book—has encouraged my body to refrain from some of the usually negative processes of aging.

I delight in deciphering and monitoring what goes on with my body, internally and externally. I can never learn enough about how to nurture and heal this earthly temple of my soul. I must assume responsibility for its maintenance, and even its upgrading, at every opportunity. Any neglect of this sacred duty of caring for my body I will live to regret. Every culture—Northern, Southern, Eastern, or Western—offers some wisdom from which I can benefit. So far, life's opportunities have steered me mostly toward the Eastern and Western principles.

I was born in the United States to Chinese parents who were foreign students. My father studied at Princeton University and then at Hartford Seminary, and when he received his Ph.D., we returned to China. My parents belonged to the first generation of Chinese who underwent the great leaps back and forth between Eastern and Western cultures.

As a two-month-old baby on a slow boat back to China, I became emaciated. My seasick mother could not continue to breastfeed me and there was no baby formula aboard. From then on, I came down with measles, whooping cough, and other infant illnesses, and my childhood was full of various medications and cod liver oil. Although I was still very young, my instinctive resourcefulness and creativity helped me to imagine two containers in my stomach: one for those awful bowls of herbal tea, cod liver oil, and pills, and the other for delicious food, especially at Grandma's house. Self-pity was overcome, and I had a happy childhood.

My paternal grandparents were among the first Christians in China, but my maternal grandmother was a devout traditional Buddhist all her life. Missionaries and Western medicine marched together hand in hand in early missionary work, and early Chinese Christians accepted the Christian God and the Western doctor as a package. In those days, being a good Christian meant defecting from the practice of traditional herbal medicine, which was being parceled up with other activities as "superstitious." I was constantly being shuttled back and forth between the extremes of the two cultures. When medical needs arose, I was looked after by both Western physicians and Chinese herbalists, taking pills and drinking those bowls of bitter herbal tea. Each of these treatments was discreetly kept from one or the other grandmother and even from friends and relatives devoted to either camp. Fortunately, my mother has always had the opened-mindedness, insight, and knowledge to balance the benefits of both medicinal concepts, and I was spared being double-dosed to death.

For me, the ancient disciplines, especially traditional practices of healing, work well with the latest vitamins, drugs, and other scientific approaches, when they are combined wisely. I see no need to choose between them.

Western medicine with its rapidly advancing scientific proofs and instruments has been the dominating authority in caring for human physical needs in Western society—and beyond. It appears to have staked out the rights to every corner of the human body, leaving not much room for medicinal benefits from other cultures to be included in the healing process.

Practitioners of Eastern traditional medicine need not feel the threat of being crowded or usurped by Western scientific medicine, or the other way around. In my mind, Western medicine is more capable of attending to my grounded form, while Eastern healing disciplines are more capable of attending to my vital form. Why should there be any conflict? My solid grounded form naturally benefits most from a solid, grounded, scientific approach that uses scientifically proven facts. The vital body, the more abstract form, yet just as dynamic, benefits from the subtlety of Eastern healing methods and practices.

At the mellow age of 50, I became gradually aware that I had spent my life getting Westernized even though I had lived many years in the East. I was depriving myself of my heritage. I decided to take up something very Chinese: the discipline of *chi kung*. The ancient Chinese practice of *chi kung* uses deep breathing in coordination with appropriate movement and meditation to generate and channel our inner *chi* energy for personal power and healing.

As I worked with this traditional practice, I gradually began to sense my body as the coming together of two forms: my grounded form and my vital form. I can switch my attention from one to the other as if I were switching TV channels. My grounded form is the one that everyone can see, the one that x-rays and MRIs can view, the one that is made of flesh and bone. My vital form I sense and see with my mind's eye as a misty, warm, rainbow-colored form, sponged up, absorbed into, and interposed with my grounded form. It's almost like floating a cloud into a very finely meshed statue. My vital form has no outer skin or boundaries, and it can shrink or expand. When I am unhealthy, its consistency can become lumpy or it can thin out or be blotchy or wrinkly. It can even disintegrate or become disconnected. This vital form is my private domain, and only those who care to make the effort can perceive its existence. With or without qualified help, I must be the one in full charge of my vital form. My grounded body is nourished on oxygen, and my vital form is nourished on *chi*. I would compare the appearance of my vital form to the cartoon figure Casper, the Friendly Ghost, except that it is more transparent, iridescent, and obscure.

Now as I head toward the second half of my sixties, my vital form is increasingly visible. In the mirror, when I concentrate, I can see my vital form exuding beyond the boundaries of my grounded form. Absolutely exhilarating! My vital form must have been blooming gradually, and now my naked eyes have been enlightened to that blossoming.

My concept of a double-form body has helped me to understand how I function as a total being. When I was younger and very busy with my performing career, perhaps I did not have the wisdom to observe beyond the physical. I was obsessed with my grounded form, as I believe most people tend to be. My mind was so overcome with sensations of my grounded form that I was oblivious to any sensations of my vital form. My grounded form had eclipsed my vital form. Now, as I allow my inner eye to search, I perceive and feel the omnipotence of my vital form.

I need not give up if my doctor should ever diagnose me as incurable or tell me that my symptoms have no basis. I will have another option. I will check my vital form and most likely find healing there.

My two forms interweave, gravitate toward one another, and even superimpose themselves on each other. They rely on each other for survival and mutual nurturing. This co-mingling and coexistence produces a physical-mental-emotional multidimensional me.

Chi *and the Vital Form*

Applying the techniques offered in *The Art of Breathing* not only boosts the supply of oxygen and cultivates *chi* energy, but it also nurtures a core center upon which my physical and mental stability can pivot.

Although *chi* is the element that Eastern medicinal principles have been built upon for thousands of years, an understanding of *chi* energy has never been established within the boundaries of Western medical science. Could it be that this subtle *chi* energy resides mainly in the vital form of a person?

About 15 years ago, while I was living in Hong Kong, my friend Elaine and her husband Sam visited us. In updating our mutual activities, Sam told me of his experience with Transcendental Meditation. His out-of-body experiences fascinated me. Shortly after that, one afternoon, when I was resting in preparation for singing the leading role in *Don Pasquale* that evening, it happened. Wanting to have an instant nap, I tried out Sam's method of relaxation. All of a sudden, I was up there looking down on me lying in bed. Unprepared for what took place, and scared, I shook my legs and came back together. I never tried that again.

Recently, without my trying, this phenomenon has resurfaced in another dimension. Why not? There is so much more of me than meets the eye. And there is so much more to unfold. I was facing the mirror doing my usual nightly exercises. I saw an aura extending beyond, framing me with a faint yellowish/pinkish hue more than an inch wide. Gradually, it grew wider and fainter, and then it dissolved into the atmosphere. During that short moment, I was enthralled and absolutely exhilarated.

I sometimes compare my physical body to a sweater knitted with yarns of two different colors, simultaneously. Let's say a pink yarn represents the vital form and a green yarn represents the grounded form. When I see a pucker in the green yarn, it may not be a fault in the green yarn. It may be a snag in the pink yarn that is causing the pucker. If I try to fix the fault by fidgeting with the green yarn, I won't be able to correct it. But if I trace and release the snag in the pink yarn, I'll fix the green pucker. In other words, a headache may not always indicate that something is wrong with your head (or your grounded body). Perhaps checking the *chi* flow of your vital body may heal the headache or a neckache or even a stomach ache.

When we cultivate the muscles of our grounded form, we develop physical strength and strong muscles. When we cultivate our vital body, we develop inner strength and vitality and cultivate character traits such as empathy, patience, understanding, sensitivity, intuition, love, and many other subtle inner qualities and strengths.

Proper breathing fills my grounded form with oxygen as it infuses the vital form with *chi* energy.

My grounded form is earthbound, but my vital form beams outward, interacting with the atmosphere. My grounded form is sex oriented, and my vital form is love oriented.

The superimposition and interaction of our two forms constitutes our physical being. The grounded form relies on oxygen and nutrition, and the vital form relies mainly on the supply, condition, and flow of *chi*. The wellness of both greatly depends upon how we breathe.

Physical exercises or disciplines also strengthen both forms. According to my experience, circular movements tend to strengthen the vital form, whereas angular or straight-line movements strengthen the grounded form.

Music or sequences of sound with rhythm affect the well-being of both my forms in various ways. That which is stimulating to my grounded form may be jarring to my vital form. I discern when and how and which sounds are most suitable and beneficial for either of my forms.

The Two Forms and Gender Identification

I like to toy with the supposition that this double form just may have an impact on the way we classify gender. We can obviously identify the female and male gender of the grounded form. Suppose the vital form has variations that do not necessarily identify us as male or female but are, rather, represented by the dominating traits of *yin* or *yang*. Traditionally, *yin* is usually associated with traits considered female and *yang* with traits considered male. In other words, the stereotypical consensus is that a female is *yin* dominated and a male is *yang* dominated. However, no single body can survive with only *yin* or *yang* traits. Every person has a mixture of both and is endowed at birth with his or her own natural spectrum of *yin* and *yang*. A formulated yin-yang combination that is considered balanced for one person may not be balanced for another.

Let me continue to play the game of supposing that my double-form body concept is credible. The possibility then exists that a male grounded form may be paired off with a *yin*-dominated vital form, or a female grounded form may be paired off with a *yang*-dominated vital form. What then? As a rule, *yin* represents the feminine principle, and *yang* represents the masculine. Therefore, for me to designate the gender of any person solely by the appearance of his or her grounded form would not be accurate. If *yin* and *yang* in the vital body should be taken into consideration in determining the degrees of a person's gender orientation, then certainly very few of us on this earth could claim that we were 100 percent pure male or female.

Certain segments of various societies throughout civilization, including some societies of today, still consider being manly or masculine to be demonstrated by hunks of muscle and brute force. In actuality, this muscular appearance pertains only to the grounded form. Considering that two forms are equally important to this one body, giving full credit to one form alone seems imprecise.

Throughout the centuries, both Eastern and Western civilization have taken their judgments and perceptions about manhood a step further. Consider the word *gentleman*. The quality of a culturally refined gentleman may frequently be considered effeminate by some. Traditional Chinese concepts define an educated, cultured, intellectual person as one who possesses more invisible brain muscles. Laborers, soldiers, and fighters, whether men or women, possess more physical muscles.

If I were to play further with my game of a double-body concept, then the reality of Nature matching a male grounded body with a *yin*-dominated vital form, or vice versa, is a possibility. All sorts of combinations are possible. The clean-cut line of the genders would become more vague and flexible. When a female grounded form is not paired off with a *yin*-dominated vital form, or a male grounded form is not paired off with a *yang*-dominated vital form, what then? The natural characteristics of the vital form will be suffocated by society's dogma, resulting in one very unhappy person—or a rebel who is ostracized.

Human beings are full of surprises. Who knows what the future will bring? One thing can be known for certain: How we breathe will always be the core of how we survive.

Breathing and the Two Forms

As we have learned, abdominal deep breathing strengthens the core. I consider the core to be the pivotal point on which both forms peg and interweave. Without the ability to practice abdominal deep breathing and establish the core, taking advantage of the double-form concept is ineffective or unworkable.

The condition of the two forms should be balanced. The overpowering or overdevelopment of the vital form undermines the stability and contentment of the grounded form. As inhabitants of this earth, the basic sensation of being sufficiently grounded is essential. However, if we allow ourselves to be overladen with this grounded sensation, we may feel stuck and depressed. By letting ourselves feel overly grounded, we forsake and deprive ourselves of the abilities that come with the vital form. These include the will and the agility to move, to rise above, to aspire, and to reach outward and upward, physically and mentally, with self-confidence. Our vital form needs to be developed sufficiently so that it is able to exude freely beyond the boundaries of the grounded form when situations call for that. Flaunting and wasting the essence of either form may leave you with empty tanks. Be kind to yourself. Be wise.

Overextending either one of the forms will take a toll on the other. We must learn how to recuperate from such an overextension. A successful performer has to overextend so as to come off bigger than life on stage. To do so makes great demands on his or her vital form. If the type of performance demands great physical skill and exertion, the performer's grounded form is overextended as well. That is why one usually has that high or let-down feeling after a performance, the sensation of being thinned out and hollowed out. I know those sensations well. I have lived through them throughout my career. Many performers—not just those who perform on stage but other great performers in the fields of business, law, medicine, and education, among others—all those who give out overabundantly what they've got in order to perform well, experience this thinned-out and hollowed-out sensation. Many performers resort to getting drunk or drugged or some other manner of numbing themselves. The wise ones unwind and compensate by doing soothing physical exercises, meditation, and relaxation to induce deep breathing and strengthen the core. They get a rapid, steady, and enjoyable recharge to both their forms. The numbing method works as a quick fix, but what it fixes will be back worse then ever each time until the performer is burned out.

Mentally upsizing or downsizing either the vital form or the grounded form can be beneficial or not, depending on the balance of the two forms and the needs of the person at the time. The size of these forms is not what you see in the mirror; they are the size that your mind and emotions perceive them to be under specific circumstances. When your grounded form feels dwarfed or shrunken, the energy of your vital form can be used to exude outward, helping to lift your grounded form out of the pit.

The boundaries or borders or the outer skin of our grounded form should always feel porous, never sealed in as though in a rubber glove. Tension frequently causes our pores to seal and imprison our vital form's ability to extend its vitality outward. Negative entities may also need to be discharged from within the grounded form, but they are prevented from being released when they are sealed in. Intentionally will those "pores" to be relaxed and ventilated at all times. Always resort to your deep breathing, and draw support from your core.

You must breathe to your core and exhale through your core to be able to accomplish the balance of grounded and vital forms that establishes you as a healthy, vibrant being. The art of breathing will bring you to this balance.

For information regarding *The Art of Breathing* book, video or boxed sets, please contact: Vivi Company, P.O. Box 750, Glendale, CA 91209-0750 U.S.A.; or, call 1-800-INHALE-8 (1-800-464-2538)/1-818-500-8889; or, send a FAX to 1-818-507-6638.

About the Author

Nancy Zi was born in the United States in 1930 to Chinese parents. Raised in China since infancy, she returned to the United States in 1949. She attended Millikin University in Illinois and was graduated with a bachelor's degree in music, majoring in vocal performance. She continued her vocal training in Chicago and New York City. She has more than thirty years of experience in teaching singing and has performed extensively as a professional vocal soloist in concerts, operas, operettas, oratorios, and television and radio programs.

Growing up in China, Nancy Zi was greatly influenced by the Eastern belief that our mental and physical well-being is governed by an inner energy called *chi*. She has been a fervent practitioner of *chi kung* for many years. Through this ancient Chinese discipline, which teaches proper handling of breath, body movements, and meditation, she has derived great benefits. With years of experience, Nancy Zi realized that the vital energy used in Western civilization for classical singing and other performances is comparable to *chi*. She found that in Western culture this inner vitality is directed outward for external accomplishments, whereas in Eastern culture it is directed primarily inward for healing and maintaining good health.

Weaving together the best of these two cultures, Nancy Zi has created *chi yi*, which literally means "the art of breathing," a new and simple way to acquire a sound breathing technique. Through the direct approach of teaching *chi yi*, the author hopes to dispel the mysticism that surrounds the generating, cultivating, and utilizing of inner energy to improve overall performance and well-being. In her book and video, *The Art of Breathing*, Nancy Zi discusses what she has learned and developed—a program of effective breathing principles accessible to an international audience.

The author and her husband of 41 years, S. Paul Li, spent much of their married life in Hong Kong, but they have now settled in Los Angeles, California. They have a son and a daughter.